DISCOVERING
VINTAGE
Washington, DC

A Guide to the City's Timeless Shops, Bars, Restaurants & More

LAURA BRIENZA

Photography by Jai Williams

Globe
Pequot

Guilford, Connecticut

The *Discovering Vintage* series was created by Mitch Broder, the author of *Discovering Vintage New York: A Guide to The City's Timeless Shops, Bars, Delis & More.*

Globe
Pequot

Distributed by NATIONAL BOOK NETWORK

Copyright © 2015 by Laura Brienza
Photography copyright © 2015 by Jai Williams

British Library Cataloguing in Publication Information Available
Library of Congress Cataloging-in-Publication Data Available

ISBN 978-1-4930-1340-1 (paperback)
ISBN 978-1-4930-1341-8 (e-book)

∞™ The paper used in this publication meets the minimum requirements of American National Standard for Information Sciences—Permanence of Paper for Printed Library Materials, ANSI/NISO Z39.48-1992.

Contents

About the Author

*L*aura Brienza is a writer from New Jersey. Her career began in Washington, DC, when she was a student at Georgetown University. As a reporter for *The Hoya,* Laura's first assignment was to cover Afghan president Hamid Karzai's visit to campus. Ever since, she's been hooked on exploring DC's unique, storied place in history. She has explored the city's many museums, hot spots, and neighborhoods as a tourist, resident, and artist. Her nonfiction has been seen in *Flavor & The Menu, Chicken Soup for the Soul,* and *20 Something Magazine.* Her plays have been developed and produced at the Kennedy Center, Lark Play Development Center, FringeNYC, Capital Fringe, Luna Stage, Midtown Direct Rep, and Off the Wall Performing Arts Center. She also writes for film and TV. In her spare time, Laura enjoys racing triathlons.

Acknowledgments

I give my deepest thanks and gratitude to my agent, Anne Marie O'Farrell, and Amy Lyons at Globe Pequot for the opportunity to write this book.

Thank you to all the owners, managers, servers, bartenders, and artists who shared their time, knowledge, food, and drink with me as I researched their establishments.

Many thanks to Jai Williams for her work on all this book's photography.

Thank you to David and Bonnie Brienza, who took me to Washington, DC, every year as a teenager, and Betsy Sheil, who drove me to check out Georgetown University one spontaneous night many moons ago. Those visits changed my life and ultimately made this book possible.

Introduction

ashington, DC, has never been cooler. The capital's restaurant scene has exploded in the last decade. Areas that I avoided during my college years at Georgetown University are now hopping neighborhoods where you can try the latest in culinary arts and nightlife. In a city where presidents revolve every four to eight years and college students infuse the population with a new crop of fresh faces every fall, change is a leading characteristic of DC.

In this sea of turnover, the constants stand out. And in the restaurant industry alone, where 90 percent of independent eateries close in the first year and the rest within five years, a restaurant that can survive decades is a veritable outlier.

In these pages, you will find restaurants, bars, and shops that have stayed open as their neighbors closed, survived while their counterparts burned, and endured while their neighborhoods changed around them.

Finding establishments in DC that qualified as "vintage" was a bit of a struggle because many businesses closed after the 1968 riots.

After Martin Luther King Jr. was assassinated on Thursday, April 4, 1968, a single brick thrown through the window of the Peoples Drug Store ignited violent riots on U Street. Those riots spread to other parts of the city. By Sunday, eight hundred fires would be started, many businesses looted and burned, twelve killed, and more than one thousand injured. More than nine hundred businesses turned to rubble. It took decades for neighborhoods to recover from the devastation.

In the following pages, you will find establishments that were spared after they hung signs that said "Soul Brother," others that owners defended with shotguns, and some that just got lucky.

Every restaurant, bar, or shop in this book has a unique story. You will meet a Vietnamese POW whose restaurant is frequented by American

POWs. You will peek inside the restaurant where the Cuban Missile Crisis was resolved over lunch. You'll sit at the booth where JFK proposed to Jackie, stroll through the lobby where the term "lobbyist" was coined, and trade recipes with the woman who opened the nation's first certified organic restaurant.

You'll learn new things about familiar faces, like the fact that George W. Bush loved Chinese food. Or that the founding fathers loved to drink Madeira.

You'll learn random things, like that minigolf has sexist origins. That Barack Obama has a cousin in Ireland. And the scientific difference between ice cream and frozen custard.

Mostly you'll meet hardworking people who have lived the American Dream by finding a demand and supplying it.

These fifty establishments have led me down so many different roads in history, politics, and culture. The NSA must have been truly puzzled by all the things I Googled while writing this book. I truly enjoyed learning the content of these pages, and I hope you enjoy reading it.

BEN'S CHILI BOWL

1213 U STREET NW • WASHINGTON, DC 20009

(202) 667-0909 • BENSCHILIBOWL.COM

A Bowl of History

There's something special about Ben's Chili Bowl. There's had to be for it to survive the race riots of 1968, the drug problems of the 1970s, five years of subway construction in the 1980s, the desegregation of DC, and the revitalization of U Street. Since opening its doors, Ben's has served an ever-changing community. But through it all, the people have spoken: we need Ben's.

After putting himself through college by working in restaurants, Ben Ali decided to open his own. His wife, Virginia, quit her job at a bank to be his partner. "I was a little frightened," she says. "But Ben said, 'We will make this work if we have to sell the car, sell the apartment, build a shower, and put a bed in the back [of the restaurant].' Of course, we didn't have to do that." They didn't, indeed: after opening on August 22, 1958, Ben's Chili Bowl would go on to be not only a successful business but an important cultural landmark.

Ben, a Trinidadian immigrant, and Virginia, who is African American, wanted to build their business in the heart of the black community, and that was U Street. At the time, U Street was known as Black Broadway. The best of the best in African-American talent performed at nearby venues and then popped into Ben's for a chili dog or burger. Nat King Cole, Duke Ellington, Miles Davis, and Ella Fitzgerald were frequent customers. DC was segregated at the time, and in addition to being a hotbed of artistic talent, U Street was home to middle-class African-American doctors, lawyers, and professionals. The restaurant became a staple in the African-American community during this time of artistic renaissance.

When you step into Ben's, you feel like you're a part of its fertile beginnings. The red booths and stools at the front counter are the same ones where these creative legends sat. Groups of five or more can enjoy table service, but most people will pay at the same counter where Martin Luther King Jr. ordered and then perch on the same stools where important developments in civil rights took place.

After Dr. King was assassinated on Thursday, April 4, 1968, riots engulfed U Street. Most businesses closed. But not Ben's. Ben and Virginia hung a sign outside that said "Soul Brother" to identify themselves as an African-American business. Rioters spared Ben's. But many of their neighbors burned.

The mayor imposed a 5:30 p.m. curfew to instill order on Friday, April 5, but Ben's secured permission from the Student Nonviolent Coordinating Committee to remain open. The Bowl became a gathering point for activists, firefighters, and public officials working to restore peace.

U Street would not really recover from the devastation of the riots for two decades. In the 1970s, middle-class black families moved out of U Street and drugs moved in.

Longtime Chili Bowl supporter Bill Cosby put Ben's on the nation's radar when he held a press conference to celebrate the success of *The Cosby Show* at the Bowl in 1983. Ben's hung a sign that read "People Who Eat For Free: Bill Cosby. No One Else."

In spite of the drugs and crime, Ben's never really struggled financially until the late 1980s, when subway construction disrupted U Street for five years. "Even my husband thought it was a waste of time [to stay open]," recalls Virginia. They scaled back to two employees and relied on faithful regulars and Metro workers to stay in business. One group of men came to the Bowl regularly after work. "They were always there, always supportive, our extended family," reflects Virginia. She bought a television so the group could watch basketball games at the Chili Bowl. It wasn't a business

Vintage Spot
Vienna Inn

Ben's Chili Bowl may get most of the press about DC chili dogs, but the Vienna Inn's also in the game: they sell ten thousand chili dogs every month. Open since 1960, this family-run Vienna landmark also rents kegs of beer if you're having a party or you're just really thirsty. Sweaty patrons welcome; this place is popular for groups after a game or cyclists after a ride.

**120 Maple Avenue E, Vienna, VA 22180,
(703) 938-9548, viennainn.com**

decision. "It was personal. For them." After construction ended, they hung a sign that said "We Survived Metro."

The Metro stop brought new customers to the Chili Bowl, and since the 1990s, Ben's has served an increasingly diverse community while remaining an important place in black culture. Bill Clinton's staff liked to take out from Ben's, and ten days before his inauguration, Barack Obama ate at Ben's. Obama became the second person to qualify for free meals at Ben's, although the sign clarifies "But he paid!"

The anchor in all Ben's history is, of course, the food. The most famous item on the menu is the Chili Half-Smoke. This mixed pork and beef sausage is grilled and topped with mustard, onions, and spicy chili. Other classics include the chili dog, chili con carne, and the chili burger. All burgers are made from never-frozen beef, and healthy options like turkey and veggie burgers are available. Ben's spicy homemade or vegetarian chili can be added to any sandwich, sausage, or burger you order. Comfort sides like fries and potato salad and desserts like milk shakes or slices of cake will fill you up.

If you want to avoid the lines at Ben's, go on a weekday in the winter. If you do end up waiting in a line that snakes outside into the adjacent alley, pass the time by admiring Aniekan Udofia's graffiti-inspired mural depicting famous Chili Bowl supporters Barack Obama, Donnie Simpson, Chuck Brown, and Bill Cosby.

Ben Ali passed away in 2009, and at eighty-one, Virginia no longer actively runs the business. But her sons, daughters-in-law, and even her grandchildren are up to the challenge. Her fourteen-year-old grandson has already said he plans to run the Bowl when he's older.

The food at the Bowl is worth your while, but being a part of this landmark's history is the real reason to make Ben's a must. The family values and communal character of Ben's Chili Bowl have made it a special place for Washington, DC, since 1958, and will undoubtedly make it thrive for years to come.

BIG PLANET COMICS

4849 CORDELL AVENUE • BETHESDA, MD 20814

(301) 654-6856 • BIGPLANETCOMICS.COM

Holy Comics, Batman!

You don't need tingling Spidey senses to tell that comics are having a moment. Actually, it's more of a decade. Since the *X-Men* series hit theaters in 2000, we've seen comic book adaptation after adaptation grace the big screen, and TV shows based on comics like *The Walking Dead* and *Gotham* have confirmed the comic industry's own superpower: profitability. In 2013, the source material that's inspired these screen successes—the comic books themselves—generated $870 million in sales.

If you want to get your hands on a comic book or graphic novel, get in your Batmobile and head for the original Big Planet Comics in Bethesda. Since 1986, Big Planet Comics has not only survived as the comic book industry has evolved, but it's expanded to three additional stores in Vienna, College Park, and U Street.

When founder Joel Pollack was home sick as an eight-year-old, his mother gave him an issue of *Superboy* titled "The Robot Boy of Smallville." It blew chicken soup out of the water. Unfortunately, Pollack's mother passed away a year later. When his father remarried, Pollack inherited a new stepbrother, and his comic collection. "I found his comics," says Pollack, and "made them mine."

Over the years, Pollack's aunt Kitty nurtured his interest in comics by introducing him to her friend Ira Schnapp, a letterer at DC Comics. Ira invited Pollack to spend time at the DC offices. He spent two memorable days shadowing artists Murphy Anderson and Curt Swan. The visit was "a

turning point in my life," states Pollack. He wanted to become a professional artist. Pollack took a few art classes, but mostly relied on reading comics to learn illustration tricks. He drew covers for *Rocket's Blast* and *Fantastic Magazine* but realized he simply wasn't good enough to earn his keep as a professional artist. "I just couldn't match the guys that I was meeting," Pollack says of the artists he met at conventions.

But he parlayed his love of comics into the next best thing: his own comic book store. Affluent and underserved, Bethesda was the perfect location. "People from Bethesda were going all the way over to Silver Spring to buy their comics." Not anymore.

The Bethesda store has changed locations three times over the years, but never by more than fifty feet. Today, a life-size inflatable Spiderman climbs on the ceiling above the new and recent releases in the neatly organized shop.

Some comic book stores get a bad rap among women for being dirty or for employing men who ogle female shoppers, but not Big Planet. Pollack is proud of the store's well-lit, clean look, which he connects to its 25 to 35 percent female clientele.

Pollack's first employee, a teenager named Greg Bennett, become his business partner. At sixty-five, Pollack has no plans to retire. But when the time comes, he expects Bennett to completely take over.

Big Planet Comics has become a fixture in the community, bringing comics lovers together. One couple even held their wedding ceremony at Big Planet in 2009. Alfredo Ignacio and Becky Kim got hitched surrounded by comics, the mutual interest that initially brought them together. "Thankfully, I've never hosted a funeral," jokes Pollack.

Every year on the first Saturday of May, Big Planet participates in Free Comic Book Day. FCBD honors comics and gets readers inside independent comic book stores. Certain comic books are available free of charge, and others are on sale. Big Planet even puts together a bag of free comics that's kid-friendly for the under-ten crowd. "We usually have a line that goes all the way down the block," says Pollack.

Comics and their sellers have gone online. Websites such as Thrillbent offer subscription packages wherein readers pay a monthly fee to peruse the site's comics collection. Pollack doesn't think that comics translate well to digital but understands his paper preference may be a product of age. "There's a new generation that's going to grow up with digital," he says. Pollack thinks the Internet has had a "mostly positive" impact on the comics industry, but that there are "certainly people who are going to buy digitally and not walk through my doors." Big Planet's foray into technology comes in the form of its Vienna and U Street locations' weekly podcast, which discusses comics across all mediums.

More than two decades ago, Pollack decided to focus on graphic novels rather than single issues. Back then, only "the best of the best" was compiled into novel editions, says Pollack. Today they're very common. Like the binge-watching trend, comic book consumers like their content in big helpings.

Big Planet's been affected by changing reader demographics. "With the advent of the popularity of video games, we lost a big segment of our readership, which was eleven- to fourteen-year-olds," explains Pollack. But comics' recent popularity with readers aged eight to eleven has helped to combat those losses.

Once relegated to the nerds, comics have become mainstream. Yes, the industry surged in the 1980s with the relaunch of series such as *The Watchmen,* and as comics became more mature, their audiences extended well into adulthood. But particularly in the last decade, comics have become cool. FOX megahit *The OC*'s protagonist Seth Cohen is at least partly responsible for the geek-chic transition. Cohen's love for comic books and his foray into authorship took up quite a lot of screen time, paving the way for future mainstream characters whose love of comics was not an example of their nerd-dom but, rather, part of their cool factor.

The millennium belongs to the Steve Jobses and Mark Zuckerbergs of the world. Whereas old comic book film adaptations were campy—think the *Batman* movies of the 1960s—today's film versions are sleek and cool. Comic book–reading geeks rule the world. "As they should," says Pollack.

Artists in the Alley

A band member's girlfriend dances alone to the beat of the band playing onstage at Blues Alley. She's grooving, clapping, and says, "That was amazing," in a brief lull between songs that everyone can hear. Thank goodness the candles on the table are fake, because she knocks one over while shaking her hips. With this kind of enthusiasm, she *must* be connected to the band. Only she's nobody's girlfriend. She's not even a sister or cousin. She's here alone, and on her way out the door, she tells a staff member, "I needed that."

For fifty years, this Georgetown jazz supper club in an alleyway off Wisconsin Avenue has been providing a stage for artists and great performances for music lovers. Every night, the club features 8 and 10 p.m. shows by a wide variety of jazz musicians. Tickets vary based on the lineup, but usually hover around $25. Operations director Kris Ross describes the atmosphere as "seedy elegance." Yes, Blues Alley is in an alleyway, but this is *Georgetown*, where people pay $3 for cupcakes and wear boat-print shorts. Granted, in the 1960s, Georgetown was more leather jacket than J.Crew, but today this is the world's safest alleyway.

A blue sign on a brick façade welcomes patrons inside, where saxophones, trumpets, and various horns hang on the exposed-brick walls. About thirty-five circular tables draped in blue tablecloths face the rectangular stage close to the action, because when somebody's playing the blues, you want to be close. Nobody goes to a jazz and blues concert at a stadium. There's a bar in the back, and waitresses serve a full Creole dinner menu to patrons meeting a $12 minimum.

On a Tuesday night, the Royal Southern Brotherhood plays on a stage bathed in blue, red, and pink lights. But for hungry and thirsty jazzheads, the menu provides plenty of options. The jambalaya, Cajun-spiced crab cakes, and shrimp over cheese grits exemplify the New Orleans–inspired menu.

Virginia-born clarinet and vibraphone player Tommy Gwaltney converted an eighteenth-century carriage house into Blues Alley in 1965. The club did not have a kitchen back then and faced competition from fellow Georgetown jazz club Cellar Door and U Street's famous Bohemian Caverns (also profiled in this book). The club employed a house band that played with soloists, and Gwaltney often had to instruct audience members to "shut up and listen."

The second owner, John Bunyan, a jazz-loving businessman, really turned Blues Alley into a profitable staple in DC's music scene in the 1970s. Bunyan did away with the house band, attracting bands, duos, trios, and more to play at Blues Alley, not just soloists. He also instituted a "Quiet, Please" policy that turned the club into a more music-focused venue. The addition of a dinner menu also kept patrons' mouths full and silent while artists showcased their talents on stage. He also introduced smaller tables to the space, preventing large groups from becoming too boisterous.

Bunyan ran the business until 2005, and his stepson Kris has been with the club for twenty years. In 2005, current owner and executive director Harry Schnipper took over. Schnipper frequented the club for decades before purchasing it a decade ago. By day he works as a real estate broker. By night he runs the city's oldest, continuously operating jazz club.

Blues Alley has provided several artists a space to record live albums. Wynton Marsalis recorded *Live at Blues Alley* with the Wynton Marsalis Quartet. Eva Cassidy recorded her own *Live at Blues Alley* album in January 1996, just ten months before her death. It went platinum.

Blues Alley has provided stages for many more artists such as guitarist Charlie Byrd, Maynard Ferguson of the Birdland Dream Band, and trumpeter Dizzy Gillespie. "Our performance schedule is top notch with a diverse selection of music," says Ross. Diverse is right: in one week, the club has featured jazz icon Ramsey Lewis, the Bowie State University Jazz Band, vocalist Donna Byrne, Jason Marsalis (of the "First Family of Jazz"), Dizzy Gillespie's protégé, ten-time Grammy winner Arturo Sandoval, and a student band from Israel.

Dizzy Gillespie is famous for spearheading the "bebop" style of modern jazz in the 1940s. The style swapped big bands and order for smaller ensembles with ample opportunities for improvisation.

Dizzy also founded the Blues Alley Jazz Society in 1985. The society operates the Blues Alley Youth Orchestra and a summer jazz camp and produces the Big Band Jam held in April during Jazz Appreciation Month. Gillespie passed away in 1993, but the society plays on, passing jazz down to the next generation.

The club has remained mostly unchanged over the years. One major change is a no-smoking policy. Gone are the days of the smoky jazz club. The policy benefits not only customers who enjoy a smoke-free environment but also the artists, especially seasoned performers who have suffered from a lifetime of secondhand smoke at gigs.

The majority of Blues Alley's customers are repeat visitors, and the club's mission to pass jazz down to youngsters seems to be working: "We've had four generations at a table," says Ross.

When talking about cities with great jazz scenes, New York, Chicago, and New Orleans typically get the love. But DC has contributed many artists and clubs to the national jazz scene. Duke Ellington, Billy Taylor, and Frank Wess are all DC natives who studied music together at Dunbar High School. While the number of jazz clubs in the city has dwindled since the years of Black Broadway (see the section on Bohemian Caverns), Blues Alley has remained. For fifty years, this club has kept jazz alive in the capital.

BOHEMIAN CAVERNS

2001 11TH STREET NW • WASHINGTON, DC 20001
(202) 299-0800 • BOHEMIANCAVERNS.COM

"The cave you fear to enter holds the treasure you seek." —Joseph Campbell

A large yellow saxophone hangs off the side of a brick building whose awning is decorated like the black and white keys of a piano. This is Bohemian Caverns, a supper club that has been an important place for jazz since 1926. Unlike Joseph Campbell, you might not be afraid to enter Bohemian Caverns, but musical treasure awaits.

World-famous musicians like Cab Calloway, Duke Ellington, and Miles Davis crooned at the Caverns in its early years, when the neighborhood was known as Black Broadway.

Today artists new and old play for crowds in the aptly named club, given because the basement club looks exactly like a cave, complete with stalactites. Musicians play before patrons seated at tables with white table-cloths and candles in the low-ceilinged, intimate space. Listening to jazz in the underground cave, you feel like you're someplace hip.

Couples dressed to the nines canoodle in dark corners, while others opt for jeans and platonic company on a Saturday night in February. I listen to the Dwayne Adell Trio warm up their fingers on the bass, piano, and drums while servers clad in all black take orders. Once they get going, this trio shows off their skill and genuine love for performing. The bass player brings his head close to the strings he plucks, the drummer wears a huge smile

Vintage Spot
THE HOWARD THEATRE

A concert venue, bar, restaurant, and nightclub, the legendary Howard Theatre has served Washington's musical needs since 1910. The theater was an integral player on Black Broadway, providing stages for Miles Davis, Cab Calloway, and Ella Fitzgerald, and then Marvin Gaye, Aretha Franklin, Lena Horne, and James Brown in later years. The theater closed after the 1968 riots but reopened in 2012 and features a gospel breakfast buffet on Sundays.

620 T Street NW, Washington, DC 20001, (202) 803-2899, thehowardtheatre.com

the entire set, and the pianist moves his shoulders rhythmically while he traverses the keys. If they could be dancing, they would be. But they settle for moving whatever body part they can while keeping the beat.

"There's some kind of energy that moves back and forth between the band and the audience," says owner Omrao Brown. "It's not one-directional." He's right. In the Cave, the musical experience is a shared one. The audience energizes the performers. The performers energize the audience.

The Cave first opened as the Club Caverns in the mid-1920s and has had a rocky history. It shut down in the 1940s but reopened in the 1950s as the Crystal Caverns. When Tony Taylor purchased the club a few years later, he renamed it the Bohemian Caverns. Unlike Ben's Chili Bowl, mentioned earlier in this book, the Cave was unable to remain open after the 1968 U Street Riots ravaged the neighborhood. It wasn't until the 1990s that the Bohemian Caverns reopened under Amir Afshar, and not until 2005, when current owner and manager Omrao Brown purchased the Cave with partners Sashi Brown and Jamal Starr, that it reclaimed its spot at the center of DC's jazz scene.

Brown made several changes to the club that brought the DC community downstairs to the Cave. He started an artist-in-residence program that gave a new artist four weeks to perform and cultivate a following. Brown saw artists playing as many gigs as possible with as many bands as possible just to get by. They were independent contractors working two hours at a time. The artist-in-residence program would give them a steady gig for a month, playing with the same people and allowing them to get ready to go into the studio to record or develop their sound.

Brown also started the Bohemian Caverns Jazz Orchestra, a seventeen-piece house band that plays every Monday night. Despite some stumbles in getting started, it's become very popular. "It's probably our third-best night of the week," Brown reckons.

Sometimes a group is so engrossed in their performance that Brown has to turn off the amps to get them to stop playing. "A lot of times an hour is not enough," he sympathizes. "But we've got to get the next show in."

The son of jazz musician and professor Leonard Brown, Omrao has always had music in his blood. "I've been listening to jazz and going to jazz since I was born," he says. Brown played trumpet in his early years, but these days his focus is helping others showcase their talents onstage. "I love listening to live music," he says. Running the Cave has also been a "reaffirming exposure to the general public," he says. "Ninety-nine percent of the people I meet, be they musicians or customers, [are] really good people."

Brown wanted to make the Bohemian Caverns, located close to Howard University, accessible to young people. Ticket prices are reasonable at approximately $15, and there is no food or drink minimum once inside. "We try to create an atmosphere where the next generation can get exposed to the music," says Brown, who adds that coming to the Cave is many patrons' first experience with live jazz music. The club's not even limited to those over eighteen. Minors can enjoy the music and food if accompanied by an adult. "We encourage people to bring their children," says Brown.

A bar in the back that is lit in blue serves drinks, while the kitchen offers a full dinner menu. There are small plates like catfish fingers or sides like sweet potato fries to nibble on, and salads, sandwiches, and entrees like jerk chicken pasta and southern shrimp and grits will satisfy hungrier stomachs. Order before the music starts if possible, because a rumbling stomach can distract even the most devoted jazz lover.

For the last decade, Brown has kept a watchful eye on the changing neighborhood. "Every corner is turning into a cookie-cutter luxury apartment building," he worries. "The wheels of change are definitely moving in a direction that there's at least a strong question mark," he says of Bohemian Caverns' future. Brown would love to buy the building that holds Bohemian Caverns to guarantee its future.

Brown has brought jazz back to U Street, but he doesn't just want his own club to succeed. At the end of the Dwayne Adell Trio's set, he takes the mic and encourages the crowd, "Please go see some live music. Even if it's not here."

THE BOMBAY CLUB

815 CONNECTICUT AVENUE NW • WASHINGTON, DC 20006

(202) 659-3727 • BOMBAYCLUBDC.COM

Bombay Bites

*J*ndian cuisine" was once an oxymoron in the United States. "Indian" and "fine dining" did not go together in the minds of Americans in the 1970s and 1980s. Ashok Bajaj sought to change that.

New Delhi–born Bajaj operated an Indian restaurant in London but wanted to found an establishment in the United States. "I wanted to explore the world," he says. After touring several cities in the States, he settled on DC. He searched for a location that would be trafficked by world travelers who understood or would be open to Indian culture and cuisine. Positioned very close to the International Monetary Fund, the World Bank, and the White House, 815 Connecticut Avenue was a perfect location.

But he had to convince the landlord, who doubted an Indian restaurant would drive in customers. "The knowledge of the cuisine wasn't there," Bajaj reflects. "India was not on the Americans' map to travel." So Bajaj flew the landlord to London and introduced him to Indian fine dining at his London restaurant. It worked. They negotiated a lease soon after. In 1988, Bajaj opened the Bombay Club and introduced DC to upscale Indian dining.

Modeled after the swanky dining establishments in India's capital, the Bombay Club offers a refined atmosphere. Mauve and taupe walls combine with low lighting to give the space an air of romance, and leaves of purples and coffee brown cover the carpet in a whimsical pattern. Elephant trunks wrap around the bar in the front, giving the space a hint of its national influence. But if you weren't eating Indian food, the decor would simply reek

of class, and the cuisine would be anyone's guess. There aren't any kitschy Indian decorations of Hindu gods, and there's no sitar playing in the background. Rather, a woman in furs plays piano, and waiters opt for black bow ties and vests rather than sherwanis.

The food from executive chef Nilesh Singhvi is truly delicious. The Bombay Club's signature appetizer, crispy kale, has a sweet, crunchy texture, and its date-tamarind chutney, onion, and yogurt dressing gives it a mouthwatering taste. The "once you pop, the fun don't stop" catchphrase came to mind when eating bite after bite of this dressed-up vegetable. But unlike Pringles, you won't feel the least bit guilty.

I have had a great many samosas in my day, but the Bombay Club's butternut squash and green pea samosas put all others to shame. And the duck kebab, seasoned with chilies, ginger, and nutmeg, has a wonderful kick that is sure to delight your taste buds.

Singhvi brings two decades of experience to the Bombay Club. He has worked at several high-profile restaurants in various Indian cities, including New Delhi's Taj Palace Hotel. Traditional Indian items like tandoori chicken and various thali, curry, and rice dishes pepper the menu. According to general manager Naresh Israni, the tandoori salmon, green chili chicken, and lamb vindalu are the Bombay Club's most popular dishes. A relatively new item, lamb shank braised in brown onion sauce, is also flying off the stove.

Bajaj has no culinary training but puts immense faith in his chefs, letting them innovate and drive the restaurant's menu. "Every once in a while, [we will feature] a theme of a certain city or place in India and all food will reflect that area," says Israni.

The Bombay Club's clientele has expanded over the years as the average American has become more interested and knowledgeable of Indian cuisine. "It's the in thing now," says Israni, who attributes some of that to Indian cuisine's healthy ingredients. "Every spice that is used in the curries has a medicinal value," he explains. "There was no pharmacy back in the day. Everything was cured through food." Indeed, the curcumin found in

Vintage Spot

ARMY AND NAVY CLUB

This private club includes mostly active and retired members of the army and navy, but civilians may join. The club dates back to 1885, and this site dates back to 1912. Features include a library with twenty thousand volumes, a gym, and several dining areas, including the Daiquiri Lounge, where the titular cocktail was introduced to the United States.

901 17th Street NW, Washington, DC 20006,
(202) 628-8400, armynavyclub.org

turmeric has been effective in fighting cancer. Curcumin also works as an antioxidant and anti-inflammatory to improve health in most organs. Ginger may ease nausea, and coriander promotes healthy digestion.

In the early days of the Bombay Club, business relied on elite Washingtonians who'd traveled to India or worked in international fields. George H. W. Bush ate at the Bombay Club in the restaurant's early days. Today younger crowds have started frequenting the Bombay Club, especially on the weekends. "The Internet has made the world a much smaller place. [It has] made us more popular in the younger generation. They want to experiment," says Israni.

Indian food has indeed become mainstream, driving a wide array of customers into the Bombay Club. Flavors that had once been confined to Indian dishes are popping up in American meals. Chefs have started seasoning burgers, burritos, and even pizzas with cumin, cardamom, and mustard seeds, expanding the nation's palate for Indian flavors. You can find naan, traditional Indian bread, at grocery stores. Naan also pops up on menus for flatbread pizzas. In general, Americans are eating more and more ethnic foods.

Bajaj helped to start this trend more than twenty-five years ago and continues to capitalize on its continuation. Building on the success of the Bombay Club, Bajaj has built an empire of restaurants in DC. To date, he owns eight restaurants and tries to visit at least one every day. The food, ambience, and service make Bajaj's first DC restaurant an elegant destination.

Gluten o'Clock

Bread. It's the "staff of life" according to the Bible and the most eaten food on the planet. Nowhere is bread more important (and delicious) than in Italy, but if you can't make it across the Atlantic, try North Capitol Street, where Catania Bakery has been baking authentic Italian bread since 1932.

Hailing from Catania, Sicily, Alfio and Marie Caruso immigrated to the United States with their four children, Grace, Samuel, Louie, and John. They started Catania Bakery by selling bread door-to-door. The business really took off when they began supplying bread to restaurants.

The Carusos lived above the bakery when it opened. At the time, the neighborhood was home to many Italian businesses and a diverse population of Italians, Jews, Irish, and African Americans. Catania is the last trace of what was once the closest thing DC had to a Little Italy.

Washington, DC, attracted relatively few Italian immigrants. New York, Boston, Baltimore, and Philadelphia had more opportunities for nonskilled laborers and Italian communities that attracted Italian immigrants in the late 1800s and early twentieth century. But skilled Italian laborers came to DC to work on construction projects for the Library of Congress, the Capitol Building, and Union Station.

In 1913, only about three thousand Italian immigrants called the capital home. They lived mostly in the Judiciary Square and Swampoodle neighborhoods, the latter an Irish community (see this book's section on the Dubliner).

The Caruso children followed in their parents' footsteps and ran the bakery until 1978, when they sold it to a family friend, Nicole Tramonte. Tramonte still owns and operates the business today. She learned the bakery business from her friend Grace Caruso. "She taught me everything," says Tramonte fondly.

Tramonte hails from France, but after marrying an Italian and purchasing an Italian bakery, "Everything I do is Italian," she laughs. Tramonte's added a slight French influence to the bakery with her flaky croissants and the "bonjour" she uses to greet customers. But everything else is as Italian as the Carusos. Tramonte makes each item by hand with the same all-natural ingredients and recipes employed by her predecessors.

Tramonte espouses a fondness for the Caruso family's history and maintains a close relationship with the last living Caruso child, one-hundred-year-old Louis. "I visit him every Saturday," Tramonte says as she explains the history behind the Caruso family memorabilia that decorates the walls. That memorabilia includes portraits of Alfio and Marie, photos of Grace, Samuel's high school diploma, Louis's "Super Sixth" World War II certificate, dog tags, war bonds, and more.

Tramonte has added her own family history to Catania's walls. A sign made by her granddaughter that reads "Celebrating 80 Years" in marker hangs above the counter, and a framed portrait of her grandson hangs proudly above the coffee station.

The bakery itself is nothing fancy. One bench and a single chair provide seating by the window. Rolling carts swaddle loaves of bread in checkered red-and-white linens. The space beyond the counter holds the oven and prep stations where the baking gets done.

Supplying restaurants remains about 95 percent of Catania's business today, but every Saturday morning from 7 a.m. to 1 p.m., the bakery opens its doors and invites the public in. That public is mostly Catania's regulars,

SEGRETARIA COMUNALE

Città' di Lawrence, Mass.

— · · —

I seguenti particolari riguardanti la nascita di *Lucio Caruso* appariscono dai Registri di Stato Civile esistenti in quest'Ufficio:

No. *1642* Data *Agosto 16-1914* Nome del Nato *Lucio Caruso*

Sesso *Maschile* colore *Bianco* Condizione *solo*

Luogo di Nascita *Lawrence* Nome dei Genitori *Alfio e Maria Navarr*

Occupazione del Padre *Panettiere* Luogo di Nascita del Padre *Italia*

Luogo di Nascita della Madre *Italia* Nome della L... *Virginia Petro...*

Data della Registrazione *15* ... *1910*

In fede di quanto sopra ho apposto la mia firma ed il ...o d'ufficio della Città' di Law-

..., Mass., questo giorno *22* del mese di *Maggio* Anno di

...o Signore Millenovecento *Diciassette*

Edoardo J. Wade
Segretario Comunale

Firmato)

"Sigillo del Comune di Lawrence, Mass.,"

La presente e' una fedele ed esatta traduzione dell'originale Inglese.

Lawrence, Mass., addi' *22 Maggio 1917*

Mariano Feda

Vintage Spot

mangialardo and sons

This cash-only Italian deli has been in business since 1953. Catania Bakery provides rolls for its popular subs. Try their signature "G" Man sub, named for the FBI agents who curated its combination of ham, salami, mortadella, pepperoni, provolone, and fontina.

1317 Pennsylvania Avenue SE, Washington, DC 20003, (202) 543-6212

a crowd of sixty-plus characters. There's Al, a retired cop who says, "Let me see your thumbprint," to see if we've met before; Carmine, a fellow New Yorker in a Mets cap who addresses me as "New York"; and Eric, who buys me a sfogliatelle but teases, "You only get it if you can pronounce it."

Every Saturday, these men gather to help Tramonte, socialize, and "solve the problems of the world," according to Al. Every Saturday, Catania becomes the bakery equivalent of *Cheers*. Customers are greeted by name and know to say "au revoir" to Tramonte as they leave with enough bread, pastries, and cookies to tide them over until next Saturday.

Al puts his grandson to work behind the counter, but he takes a break to show off his jujitsu skills to the small group of customers to prove "Grandpa's not tougher than me."

The regulars have an informal hierarchy. Al's at the top with behind-the-counter privileges, although Nicole claims he just "put himself there." Carmine's on deck, and Eric works the floor. "It's free help," Tramonte says of her friendly volunteers.

Business suffered after the 2008 recession, when restaurants cut back on offering free bread and as soft bread became trendy. Catania specializes in hard, crusty bread. Made without preservatives, it has a short shelf life. And as the gluten-free diet sweeps the nation, people are also eating less bread than before. But as a supplier of restaurants and delis in DC, Maryland, and Virginia, Catania continues to serve the bread needs of many. "I love to be around food," says Tramonte. Judging by her collection of regulars, the feeling is mutual.

The neighborhood has changed like so many DC communities thanks to an infusion of young professionals. It has also become safer. "I used to hear gunshots all the time," says Tramonte. When she took over Catania in 1978, crime scene tape was a common sight on the block.

Today the atmosphere makes Catania Bakery a must-visit destination. It's a throwback to a simpler time, before coffee chains and drive-thrus. When I brought my computer with me to Catania, Eric remarked, "That's the first laptop I've seen in here." Don't come here to munch on biscotti and stare at your MacBook. Come here to make eye contact and swap stories with Italian aficionados. You might not solve the problems of the world, but you'll definitely enjoy yourself.

CHINATOWN EXPRESS

746 6TH STREET NW • WASHINGTON, DC 20001

(202) 638-0424 • CHINATOWNEXPRESSDC.COM

Putting the China in Chinatown

Clyde's of Gallery Place. Cuba Libre. Rosa Mexicana. Believe it or not, these are all restaurants in DC's Chinatown, an area that has become decreasingly Chinese over the years. But one authentic Chinese restaurant has stood the test of development: Chinatown Express.

For twenty-five years, this family-run restaurant has been providing DC's Chinese and non-Chinese population with its trademark *lai mein* noodles. Meaning "hand-stretched," chefs make *lai mein* noodles by stretching a thick rope of dough until it snaps into many strands of noodles. Standing outside, you can sometimes spy a chef making these noodles in the window. The noodles then make their way into soups and dishes at Chinatown Express and are truly special. So clearly fresh, thick, and satisfying, the noodles prove that you shouldn't judge a book by its cover. Because Chinatown Express is more of a greasy chopstick than an inviting restaurant.

Although it's located on the ground floor, Chinatown Express feels more like a basement. Bars cover the windows, and menu items written on neon pink, yellow, green, and red poster board give the space the same feel as a high school cafeteria. But the food is great and, true to its name, comes out very quickly. My order of noodles and pork came in approximately five minutes.

The mostly Chinese staff wear red polo shirts and serve patrons in the restaurant's two rooms at marbled green tables. Servers give each table a generous pot of tea and, of course, after-meal fortune cookies. On a spring afternoon, mine counseled, "The best men are molded of their faults," a comforting proclamation for all of us imperfect beings.

The menu offers plenty of classic and satisfying Chinese food like egg rolls, egg drop soup, and fried rice. The *siu lim bao*, steamed dumplings filled with pork and broth, should be eaten whole to absorb all the broth in one bite. Eight pieces of these "juicy little buns" come for just under $6. Congee (rice porridge) and noodle dishes join vegetable, meat, and seafood options. Many casseroles are also available, including an oyster, ginger, and spring onion casserole and a chicken and black mushroom casserole. Several egg foo yong dishes, the Chinese version of an omelet, are also on the menu.

If you don't know what to order, or simply can't choose, let Chinatown Express choose for you: the restaurant offers "family dinners" that serve parties of four, six, or eight people and include a wide variety of dishes. For example, one family dinner for six starts with wonton soup and egg rolls and then brings steamed pork buns, chicken lo mein, a pepper steak, roast pork with broccoli, General Tso's chicken, and shrimp egg foo yong to the table.

Some argue that the establishment of Chinatowns came as a result of self-segregation's appeal in the context of racism. This argument has merit: an 1877 joint report from the Senate and House of Representatives listed the Chinese in America as "demoralizing and degrading to our people," and the 1882 Chinese Exclusion Act famously barred new Chinese from entering the country and Chinese residents already in the United States from becoming citizens.

DC's first Chinatown was located in what is now the Federal Triangle. When Big Brother seized the land and erected seven major government buildings in 1931 (for the IRS, Commerce Department, and Justice Department, among others), Chinatown dissipated. A new Chinatown emerged on H Street between 5th and 7th Streets, but fizzled by the early 1980s as many Chinese residents moved to other parts of the city or out to the suburbs.

The next concentration of Chinese residents occurred in present-day Chinatown, from Pennsylvania Avenue to Massachusetts Avenue between 4th and 10th Streets. The construction of the Wah Luck House, a low-income building for Chinese Washingtonians, aimed to keep Chinese people *in* Chinatown. Even though much of the area has been developed by non-Chinese businesses, an ordinance requiring businesses to add Chinese characters to their signs has maintained the neighborhood's Chinese look. Starbucks, Chipotle, and Subway are just a few of the chain restaurants that have signs in both English and Chinese.

In 1986, the addition of the Gateway Arch solidified this geographic area as DC's official Chinese community. Beijing and DC decided to build the arch together after they became sister cities. But the project rubbed some Americans the wrong way: opponents wanted the arch to be American made, especially immigrants who had ties with Taiwan instead of China. These dissidents planned to erect their own arch sans Communist dollars, but the project never materialized. So under the direction of architect Alfred Liu, the twenty-eight-ton arch took shape with the cooperation of both Chinese and American laborers. Liu used the Chinese technique *dougong* to build the arch, meaning that instead of nails, the arch employs interlocking wooden brackets to secure the structure. After the massacre at Tiananmen Square in 1989, DC severed ties with its sister city. City council chairman David A. Clarke hung a black cloth on the arch to mourn the victims of the attack.

Since then, the arch has remained relatively controversy-free, although one of the arch's 280 painted dragonheads did fall off in 1990. Luckily, the one-hundred-pound head didn't injure anyone. In 2009, painters retouched the archway, and it stands beautified to welcome visitors into Chinatown on H Street between 6th and 7th.

This Chinatown seems poised to stay, and if you're looking for an authentic Chinese culinary experience, head for the red door and green awning marked Chinatown Express.

Round-the-Clock Delight

J t's more fun to eat in a saloon than drink in a restaurant." This philosophy guided Stuart Davidson as he opened Clyde's in 1963. The establishment would go on to become a Georgetown landmark and the first of many restaurants in DC's reigning restaurant empire, Clyde's Restaurant Group.

After graduating from Harvard, Davidson abandoned life as an investment banker to open Clyde's in a space previously home to a rough 'n' tough biker bar. He named the restaurant after the River Clyde in Scotland and told his wife he'd get a "real" job after selling it. He never did.

A year before Clyde's opened in 1963, the law had changed in Clyde's favor: customers could now buy liquor standing up at bars. A visual so synonymous with the idea of a bar today was once off-limits. Between 1917 and 1962, hard alcohol could be sold only to patrons seated at tables.

Six months after opening, Davidson hired John Laytham as a dishwasher. Laytham was an undergraduate at Georgetown's School of Foreign Service looking for extra cash to woo pretty girls. But he got a lot more than pocket money: he quickly rose through the ranks and became a co-owner alongside Davidson. Laytham suggested Clyde's should be open for business on Sundays—a no-go in those days. Sunday brunch and drinking while standing up—two practices commonplace today—revolutionized the dining experience at Clyde's and helped the restaurant to prosper.

By 1968, Laytham was the general manager of Clyde's. That year the restaurant made $250,000 in sales. By 1970, that figure jumped to more than a million dollars. With business booming, Davidson and Laytham had established the base they needed to expand. They started building their kingdom:

The duo purchased the Old Ebbitt Grill in 1970 (also profiled in this book), opened several other Clyde's chains, purchased 1789 and the Tombs (also profiled in this book), and opened twenty-four-hour food and entertainment complex the Hamilton in 2011. But Clyde's is what started it all: an old-fashioned bar and red booths make up the front room, which leads into additional dining rooms. Antique prints of athletic and aviation endeavors decorate the walls. Bartenders and servers wear khakis, button-down shirts, and ties, achieving a preppy look that complements the expensive, collegiate neighborhood.

If you're craving not just one omelet but a *room* full of omelets, you're a few decades late: there was once an epic room devoted *only* to serving omelets. But as the nation grew cholesterol-conscious, the policy had to go. (Ron Swanson has petitioned for its return ever since.) The room still exists, but you can order as you please there now.

People from all over DC visit Clyde's, situated on busy, upscale M Street, after shopping or lobbying for bills on the Hill. Georgetown and George Washington Universities are also nearby, so you can frequently spot parents treating their children to a meal at Clyde's. (My own mother treated me to at least one meal at Clyde's while I attended Georgetown.)

In addition to introducing DC to Sunday brunch, Clyde's was ahead of the curve when it started a farm-to-table initiative before that term became catchy. "It started with wanting a fresh tomato to go with a hamburger," explains general manager David Del Bene. To fill that demand, John Laytham worked with Clyde's Restaurant Group to start the Clyde's farm-to-table program, which brings locally sourced, fresh ingredients to all of Clyde's restaurants.

Clyde's serves classic American food. Burgers and sandwiches make up a decent portion of the menu. Other entrees include mushroom ravioli, salmon, crab cakes, and rib-eye steak. The brunch menu churns out classics like buttermilk biscuits and omelets but offers more unique items like red quinoa crepes as well.

The bar features seasonal cocktails and classic ones, from a martini made with Bombay Sapphire gin and dry vermouth to a Manhattan made with Michter's single-barrel rye, sweet vermouth, and Angostura bitters.

The "Afternoon Delights" section of the menu, which offers bites between 4 and 7 p.m., inspired the Starland Vocal Band's 1976 hit song "Afternoon Delight." Band member Bill Danoff penned the Grammy-winning number after he noticed the midafternoon items listed as afternoon delights when dining at Clyde's. From 4 to 7 p.m., you can enjoy your own PG-rated afternoon delights for about $7.

Clyde's has been in business for fifty-five years, and Del Bene is confident that it will operate for another fifty-five. "We pride ourselves on repeat business," Del Bene says. "Taking care of customers is paramount." Clyde's motivates good service in part by promoting from within. When hiring a server, David thinks long term, an approach that's been in play since Laytham rose from dishwasher to CEO. Comparably, Del Bene started as a food runner. Most of the restaurant group's executives also climbed the rungs en route to their current positions of power.

It's practically impossible to avoid Clyde's Restaurant Group if you live or eat in DC. Even the hip, huge entertainment and dining complex that is the Hamilton is rooted in this neighborhood restaurant. Clyde's advertising materials use the logo "Where patriots of all stripes come to dine" alongside a cartoon of a donkey (Democrat) and an elephant (Republican) clinking beer and martini glasses over a gregarious meal. It seems like talking across party lines has never been *less* popular, but Clyde's relaxed, upscale, congenial environment would be the ideal place for opposing sides to talk things out.

Says Del Bene, "People want an original, and Clyde's is certainly that."

CRISFIELD SEAFOOD

8012 GEORGIA AVENUE • SILVER SPRING, MD 20910

(301) 589-1306 • CRISFIELDSEAFOOD.COM

Small-Town Seafood

I'm not the owner," a woman at the front desk tells me. "I just look that way because I'm old and bitchy." She's one of several white-haired waiters and waitresses at Crisfield Seafood, a neighborhood fish joint that's been shucking clams since 1945. Some of these employees have been here for three or four decades. As Silver Spring has grown, they've seen Crisfield's stay the same.

Two rooms—one square, the other long and rectangular—make up this family-run dive. The first contains a large, rectangular bar. Customers park themselves on black-cushioned stools (some bearing large rips). Servers in white aprons dish out food and jokes in the middle. A gumball machine is tucked into a corner, along with an American flag, a bowl of pinecones, and a scale that promises to tell your weight *and* your fortune. Blue-and-white-checkered half curtains on the front windows make the space feel like your grandmother's house. Pictures of famous guests like Chuck "The Godfather of Go-Go" Brown and blues musician Memphis Gold line the wall.

The second, long, narrow room contains tables and a collection of framed antique plates inspired by various forms of sea life. Lobster claws sandwich a clock. The atmosphere is "retro kitsch," laughs general manager Bonnie Landis Swanson, finding the idea of a purposeful atmosphere rather absurd. "We haven't changed since 1945."

Crisfield Seafood opened under the leadership of Landis family matriarch Lillian Landis. "She was a quintessential businesswoman at a time when women were mostly homemakers," Swanson says of her grandmother with admiration. Landis believed in equal treatment and second chances. She once hired a man fresh out of prison for manslaughter. "He deserved a second chance," Swanson says of her grandmother's reasoning. On another occasion, Landis refused to give the mayor of Silver Spring special treatment. "There was a mayor who wanted a reservation," recalls Swanson. But Crisfield's doesn't take reservations. "She said, 'I don't care who it is. We don't take reservations' . . . [She was] fair all the way around." At Crisfield's, the small and tall are treated alike. Under Landis, Crisfield's was also one of the first restaurants in Silver Spring to integrate. On a Friday night this winter, an even mix of black and white customers ate at the restaurant.

Although not an outgoing person at home, when working, Landis transformed into a confident, feisty leader. One night a robber knocked her to the floor. As he took money from the register, Landis asked him to leave her some fives and ones. She would need to make change. Swanson sees similar qualities in herself. Reserved at home, she comes out of her shell at work. "It's like being on stage," she posits.

Despite hailing from the countryside and knowing little about seafood, Landis bought Crisfield's with the vision to support her family. The restaurant had opened in 1939 under Captain White (of several Captain White seafood businesses). In 1945, Landis purchased the restaurant and kept the name but put her own stamp on it.

In 1988, Crisfield's tried to expand to a second location, but the venture failed. The owners expected to lose their lease on the original property. They planned for this second location to become the business's sole enterprise. However, they *didn't* lose their lease. Just eight blocks away, the second restaurant failed to bring in new customers. It also lacked Crisfield's trademark lived-in vibe. Regulars who tried it came right back to the original. "People weren't ready for any kind of change," reflects Swanson. Today customers point out even the slightest change at Crisfield's to Swanson, like the addition of a wreath or even a small trinket. The family is happy to operate just one location. "When you stay small, you have more control," says Swanson, and more control means better quality.

The menu at Crisfield Seafood (obviously) revolves around seafood. The seafood bisque and the baked stuffed shrimp are the most popular dishes. The Imperial Crab is Landis's recipe. The dish bakes lumps of crab-meat in Hellmann's mayonnaise, green bell pepper, and onion. Most entrees cost around $25. Of course, specialties like the one-pound lobster tail will set you back $49. The menu includes a diverse selection of sea life, including flounder, scallops, oysters, and soft-shell crabs, in addition to soups like clam chowder and oyster stew. Land-lovers dragged here with fish enthusiasts can eat the pan-fried chicken or combine side dishes like baked potato, applesauce, and fries to make a meal.

Landis passed away in 1999, but the restaurant continues under the management of her family. Swanson's brother David works as a kitchen manager, and her cousin Jan does the payroll. Beyond blood, the staff feels like family as well. "I have employees that have worked for me for forty-two years," says Swanson. "When somebody's got difficulties, we all as a group—not just the owners, not just the management—all embrace that person."

Just like Crisfield's owners and employees, the clientele goes back for generations. "We're seeing families that came [to Crisfield's] back in 1945 [come in] with their children and grandchildren," says Swanson. Customers flock to Crisfield's from DC, Silver Spring, Annapolis, and Virginia.

Sixteen years after her passing, Landis's vision to take care of her family is clearly alive and well. So walk the half mile from the Silver Spring Metro station and take a seat at the bar.

THE DUBLINER

NUMBER FOUR F STREET NW • WASHINGTON, DC 20001

(202) 737-3773 • DUBLINERDC.COM

Get Your Guinness On

O n St. Patrick's Day, a huge delivery truck parks outside the Dubliner. The truck is full of Guinness in case the Irish pub runs out. "We empty it every year," says Gavin Coleman, the second-generation owner.

Gavin's father, Danny Coleman, opened the Dubliner in 1974. He'd come to Washington about a decade earlier. "The city was bursting with really savvy Irish people, but there was no good Irish bar," says Danny. He fixed that.

The Dubliner's in a fitting location, steps away from Union Station. The neighborhood was once known as Swampoodle, home to Irish immigrants who fled Ireland's devastating potato famine in the second half of the nineteenth century. The name comes from the term "swamp puddle," used to describe the swampy section of land. The construction of Union Station in the early years of the twentieth century forced many Irish immigrants to move away, and Swampoodle faded. But on the corner of F and North Capital, the Irish by blood or spirit can grab a pint and embrace their heritage.

Traditional Irish lettering spells out the pub's name on a green awning. Irish and American flags fly over the entrance. A long bar with green stools occupies the first floor, and Irish music flows through the other rooms that connect the restaurant in a lopsided circle. Since opening, the Dubliner has also featured live Irish music every night.

Danny's parents both came to America in the early twentieth century. His mother came legally, and his father's family "snuck in through Canada,"

Danny says. "Every time we look him up we end up in a jail," he laughs. Danny grew up in an Irish neighborhood, went to Catholic schools, and has been bleeding green his whole life. He has made about forty trips to Ireland and passed down a love for the homeland to his children. But Gavin was the best fit to take over the business. Not only did he love Ireland as much as his father did—he's made about twenty trips and got married at a castle in Ireland—but after working in both the restaurant and investment banking industries, he had the experience to lead.

"I've done every job [here] except in the kitchen," says Gavin. As a youngster, he washed dishes and worked as a server, and after graduating from college and working in New York and Italy, he returned to DC. Danny asked his son, "What are you going to do now?" Gavin replied, "I want your job." In his first act as the new GM, Gavin saved the Dubliner $30,000. "He said, 'I just canceled all the Yellow Pages advertising,'" recalls Danny, who wondered, "How the hell are people going to find us?" That hasn't been a problem, as the Dubliner is usually packed.

The most prominent patron is Barack Obama, who chose to celebrate St. Patrick's Day at the Dubliner in 2012 with his eighth cousin Henry Healy, who hails from Moneygall, Ireland. The pub usually sells 120 kegs' worth of Guinness on the holiday, and three years ago, at least one pint went to the president of the United States. Danny and Gavin had a twenty-minute heads-up that the commander in chief would be stopping by. POTUS shook hands and paid for a pint. After he downed his Guinness, the crowd started chanting "Four more beers! Four more beers!" He didn't order four more beers, but he did win four more years.

Other prominent guests of the Dubliner have included Hillary Clinton, Newt Gingrich, and Tip O'Neill. The Dubliner also gets its fair share of congressional members and staffers.

When Bill Clinton held meetings in DC for Protestants and Catholics during the Irish Peace Process to resolve conflict in Northern Ireland, both sides ended up at the Dubliner. When Danny asked representatives from both sides how often they went to church, both sides answered sparingly. "I said, 'I've been sitting with you for over a week, and I don't know who's the Protestant and who's the Catholic,'" Danny recalls telling members of the peace talks as they drank pints of Guinness with each other. Danny claims, "We're totally responsible for the peace settling in Ireland."

Over the years, the Dubliner has evolved while remaining true to its core intention to serve authentic Irish food and drinks in a relaxed Irish atmosphere. Most notably, the surroundings have changed. "This was a pretty rough neighborhood," says Danny of the area in the late 1960s. In addition to being safer, the pub has become more of a restaurant and less of a pub. In the beginning, the Dubliner sold "80 percent booze," calculates Danny. But today, father and son reckon the Dubliner sells 65 percent food and 35 percent booze. The menu includes Irish favorites like fish-and-chips and shepherd's pie, burgers, sandwiches, steak, and fish.

Guinness remains the drink of choice. "It's like looking at the U.S. military versus the rest of the world," says Gavin. "The gap is so big between [Guinness and our] other sellers." There's even a Guinness burger on the menu that consists of a beef patty marinated in Guinness and served atop a potato pancake. The pub serves other Irish beers along with local craft beers. As DC has become more posh, the Dubliner's also created a cocktail program, including an impressive whiskey list.

Gavin mainly runs the operation today, but Danny, who owns the Phoenix Hotel connected to the Dubliner, can be found at the Dubliner enjoying lunch daily. "We don't really worry about making money," says Danny. Gavin quickly interjects, "I do." But they agree that if patrons have a good time at the Dubliner, they'll come back. For forty-one years, customers have been doing just that.

EAST POTOMAC GOLF COURSE AND LANGSTON GOLF COURSE

972 OHIO DRIVE SW • WASHINGTON, DC 20024 • (202) 554-7660
26TH STREET AND BENNING ROAD NE • WASHINGTON, DC 20002
(202) 397-8638 • GOLFDC.COM

> "To find a man's true character,
> play golf with him."
> —P. G. Wodehouse

For a long time in the United States, only white men could follow P. G. Wodehouse's advice. Women could not golf because it was considered uncouth to sweat, and segregation forbade African Americans from accessing many golf courses in this country. But necessity is the mother of invention. For a group of excluded women, necessity led to the creation of minigolf. And for black Washingtonians, exclusion led to the creation of the Langston Golf Course, originally a course for minorities.

In the nineteenth century, engaging in strenuous recreational activity was considered unladylike, so playing golf was out of the question for the fairer sex. But in 1867, a golf club in St. Andrews, Scotland, found a way to get women on the green. They created a miniature golf course so that women could enjoy the game without breaking a sweat and wouldn't have to swing their golf clubs back beyond their shoulders—considered taboo. These gentle, breakable women would only have to putt. And so minigolf was born.

The game grew in popularity, especially in America. One of the oldest minigolf courses in the country—perhaps *the* oldest (the historical records aren't certain)—is located in the shadows of the Washington Mall at the East Potomac Miniature Golf Course. Dating back to about 1930, this minigolf course was part of a national exuberance for the young sport.

In the early years of minigolf, very different materials made up the green, from cottonseed hulls to ground seaweed and asbestos. During the Great Depression, minigolf also became wackier, evolving from straightforward putting holes to holes that included odd, challenging, or even frightening obstacles. On a course in Flushing, Long Island, one hole required players to hit their ball through a cage containing a live bear.

As an activity that people of all ages, genders, and income brackets could afford, minigolf soared in popularity over the first half of the twentieth century. During the Great Depression, it wasn't uncommon to see found materials like rain gutters and tires adorning courses. In the 1950s, minigolf courses fell into two camps: serious or zany. Putt Putt Golf and Games' courses took the serious approach, featuring straight putts that relied on skill. Oppositely, Al Lomma's Lomma Enterprises created now-classic obstacles like rotating windmills and moving ramps that injected luck into the game.

East Potomac Park dates back to 1912, when Congress began appropriating funds to build the park and its nine-hole golf course. The greens replaced about fifty acres of cornfields and scrub-willow. By 1917, the East Potomac Golf Course was Washington, DC's first professionally designed golf course under Walter J. Travis, a national champion on the amateur circuit who designed forty-eight golf courses during his life. The course opened to the public in the summer of 1920. In the first year of operation, 40,373 players took advantage of the twenty-five-cents-per-round price and golf facilities. In 1923, 1924, and 1930, the park added nine holes for a total of thirty-six holes. East Potomac's eighteen-hole minigolf course falls

into Putt Putt's simple, skill-focused camp. At $6 for kids and $7 for adults, it's an affordable, fun activity for the whole family.

Black Washingtonians could not golf at East Potomac or the city's other golf facilities. Only caddies got around the whites-only rule, playing rounds of golf on "caddy days" or when business was slow.

Two golf clubs, the all-black, all-male Royal Golf Club and the all-black, all-female Wake Robin Golf Club, worked to increase golf facility access to all. The Wake Robin Golf Club petitioned Secretary of the Interior Harold Ickes to desegregate the capital's golf facilities. He countered by creating a separate all-black golf course. Named the Langston Golf Course, this segregated course opened in 1939 and was named for John Mercer Langston, the founder of Howard University's Law Department and the first black congressman in Virginia.

While the RGC and the WRGC were pleased that black golfers had a facility to play golf every day of the week, a segregated facility still promoted inequality. The groups kept petitioning for desegregation, and it worked: in 1941, Ickes ordered all golf courses to admit players of any background.

With the exception of Tiger Woods, black golfers have not played a major role in the media's narrative about golf. But African Americans have a rich history with the sport that goes back well before Woods. In 1896, seventeen-year-old John Shippen placed sixth in the U.S. Open. White players boycotted the half-black, half–Native American teenager's participation, but the U.S. Golf Association's president backed Shippen. He won $10 and went on to play five more opens.

Thirteen years later, black dentist George Grant invented the golf tee. Before his invention, golfers pinched wet sand together to create a makeshift tee. This process annoyed Grant, so he invented the golf tee, which earned him patent number 638,920 on December 12, 1899. And in 1961, the same year the PGA dropped its "white-only" rule, Charlie Sifford became the first African American to earn a PGA card.

Vintage Spot

HARRY S. TRUMAN BOWLING ALLEY

On April 25, 1947, Truman knocked down seven pins to inaugurate the Harry S. Truman Bowling Alley in the White House. Eisenhower relocated the two-lane bowling alley to the Old Executive Office Building to make room for a mimeograph room, which eventually became the Situation Room. Today the Harry S. Truman Bowling Alley is used by presidents, federal workers, and their friends. If you have a contact at the White House, you too can bowl like a boss.

1650 Pennsylvania Avenue NW, Washington, DC 20502

Although Langston welcomes golfers of any race, the course continues to attract mostly African-American clientele. Famous players over the years have included Herman Boone, Joe Louis, Jim Thorpe, Charlie Sifford, and Calvin Peete. One prominent golfer the course hopes to attract: President Obama. But he has yet to schedule a tee time.

Before or after a tee time, you can enjoy a meal at the Langston Club-house Grille. The menu features breakfast, lunch, and dinner at very reasonable prices.

The East Potomac Mini Golf Course and Langston Golf Course provide ties to the history of two historically disenfranchised groups as well as a fun afternoon.

FILOMENA RISTORANTE

1063 WISCONSIN AVENUE NW • WASHINGTON, DC 20007

(202) 338-8800 • FILOMENA.COM

An Italian Hoarder's Paradise

*M*any people like to decorate for the holidays. JoAnna Filomena *loves* to decorate. For *every* holiday.

Her Italian restaurant in Georgetown is famous for its extravagant decorations that cover every inch of the basement space. If a hoarder could channel clutter into interior design, the result would be Filomena.

At the entrance to this basement gem, "Pasta Mamas" in white aprons and crocheted hairnets crank out homemade pasta in a display window surrounded by knickknacks that set the tone for Old World Italy. As you descend the stairs into the restaurant, dim lighting, Italian music, and an aesthetic overdose of decorations wake up your senses.

At Christmastime, five thousand ornaments and ten thousand lights decorate an enormous Christmas tree inside the restaurant. For Valentine's Day, pink flowers, statues of Cupid, and birds carrying hearts take over Filomena. At Easter, eggs and bunnies descend on the space, and at Halloween, skeletons, bats, and goblins raise the spook factor. Even the most intense Scrooge would find him or herself filled with holiday spirit, even for the briefest of moments. It's organized chaos that pays tribute to the owner's mother, Filomena Filomena.

Filomena believed in celebrating every holiday to the fullest and making every meal special. Lovingly prepared Italian meals were paired with white tablecloths, centerpieces, and decorations. The devoted homemaker wanted

FILOMENA

FILOMENA
RISTORANTE
Established

For Over
30
YEARS
Since 1983

to create a home that would provide a comfortable escape from the world's outside pressures. JoAnna grew up without television. Her parents focused on family and home life. JoAnna inherited her mother's caretaking gene but has applied it to a whole restaurant. She maximizes her mother's love for the holidays at Filomena by creating a whimsical, stress-free flight of fancy.

JoAnna moved from New York to Washington, DC, in 1980 to be close to her mother, whose health was in decline. She longed for an Italian restaurant that valued mealtime the way her own mother had. So after a few years of planning, she opened her own restaurant that would do just that. On May 23, 1983, Filomena opened, named for JoAnna's mother and her approach to Italian dining.

JoAnna decorated the restaurant with her mother's actual possessions. The kitchen, visible to patrons through white latticework, displays an ornate chandelier of green and purple glass hanging above Filomena's kitchen table, seating eight. Knickknacks and hanging plants fill up the space in this display kitchen and the restaurant. The music playing overhead attempts to replicate the music that JoAnna's father liked to play on his concertina (an instrument in the accordion and harmonica families).

President Obama and President Clinton have both enjoyed meals at Filomena. Clinton's visit was more controversial. At a 1994 summit in Brussels, Clinton greeted German chancellor Helmut Kohl by joking, "I was thinking of you last night, Helmut, because I watched the sumo wrestling." Even though he made this comment in the years before Internet memes, it was still a well-known faux pas. But Kohl brushed it off and invited Clinton to his favorite Italian restaurant: Filomena.

Maureen Dowd referred to the meal as "pasta diplomacy." Although it's usually just for show, the heads of state sat at Filomena's kitchen table below the grape chandelier and ordered dish after dish, both displaying their love of food. Clinton, after all, is infamous for ending his runs at McDonald's. A picture of Kohl and Clinton chowing down hangs on the wall behind the table.

Kohl's favorite dish at Filomena is the Gnocchi della Mamma. The dish combines gnocchi made by the Pasta Mamas with a Bolognese sauce that melds beef, veal, vegetables, wine, and tomatoes. The menu also offers ravioli, rigatoni, linguine, and cannelloni. U2's Bono enjoyed the rigatoni con salsicce—a marriage of rigatoni and sausage sautéed with mushrooms, onions, Chianti wine, and herbs in tomato sauce—so much that he ordered seconds.

Other famous palates that Filomena has satisfied over the years include Goldie Hawn, George H. W. Bush, Hillary Clinton, Dustin Hoffman, Chuck Norris, Billy Crystal, Ronald and Nancy Reagan, Oliver Stone, and Carmelo Anthony, who noshed on the misto di mare, a shrimp, scallop, clam, mussel, and calamari pasta dish.

The tortelloni di Michele won the People's Choice Award at the Taste of Georgetown in 2010. The dish combines tortellini stuffed with beef braised with wine and vegetables and a sauce that blends pine nuts, sage, mushrooms, and veal stock.

Veal and chicken dishes round out the entree selections, including Italian classics like chicken parmigiana and osso buco.

Filomena prepares all of its desserts in-house. Tiramisu is obviously on the menu, along with a wide selection of cakes. The hazelnut dacquoise infuses hazelnut and dark chocolate mousse into a hazelnut and meringue cake, and the mixed fruit cheesecake is the result of more than thirty recipe tweaks.

The wine list also offers many Italian wines from regions such as Sicily and Tuscany.

Although Mother Filomena's kitchen usually hosts VIPs, non-heads of state can enjoy the Old World charm of the antique kitchen for a price. Parties of at least four can pay $155 a head for a three-course meal in the room. However, it's completely possible to experience the charm and vision of this warm Italian restaurant without dropping a fortune. Just take a look around, inhale the holiday spirit, and bite into a hearty Italian entree.

FLORIDA AVENUE GRILL

1100 FLORIDA AVENUE NW • WASHINGTON, DC 20009

(202) 265-1586 • FLORIDAAVENUEGRILL.COM

Good for the Soul Since 1944

Soul food. The term conjures images of black-eyed peas, catfish, collard greens, and, in DC, the Florida Avenue Grill.

Lacey and Bertha Wilson founded the Florida Avenue Grill in 1944. It is credited as the oldest soul food restaurant in the world. Theirs were truly humble beginnings: seating consisted of just two stools, and they stayed in business "two chickens at a time." Money was so tight that the couple would serve two chickens, then use the revenue to buy two more over and over. But business eventually took off, and the Grill became a popular spot in the 1950s and 1960s for the U Street crowd after taking in concerts or shows, particularly with the African-American population during DC's days of segregation.

The Grill survived the 1968 riots thanks to Lacey. He stayed up every night at the Grill with a shotgun to protect his diner and put out a firebomb that was thrown at the building. Lacey and Bertha's son, Lacey Jr., took over in the 1970s. He expanded the Grill by purchasing the properties connected to its building and continued its tradition of cooking home-style soul food.

Today six rickety booths and eighteen red, backless stools at a very long counter make up this greasy spoon on the corner of Florida and 11th. Framed headshots of famous guests like Chris Rock, Jesse James, Queen Latifah, and Jimmy Witherspoon line the walls against the booths and above the register. Wilting flowers fill narrow circular vases at each booth, and the Cardozo Education Campus can be seen across the street through wide octagonal windows.

The menu, which offers breakfast all day, includes comfort foods like fried catfish with eggs and buttermilk biscuits smothered in sausage gravy. Dinner options range from a southern pan-fried chicken to pig's feet. Everything comes with a corn muffin and classic sides like collard greens, green beans, candied yams, and mashed potatoes. I'm partial to the Grill's potato salad, spiced up perfectly with paprika.

Nothing has been removed from the original menu, but healthy choices like sugar-free syrup and turkey sausage have been added, bringing the Florida Avenue Grill's classic style into the health-conscious modern age.

The diner is as unpretentious as its menu. The friendly staff treats everyone the same at this hash house. Famous actors like *Entourage*'s Adrian Grenier have had to wait for hours to get in on especially busy days.

In 2005, Lacey Jr. sold the Florida Avenue Grill to businessman Imar Hutchins. In truth, Hutchins was more interested in developing condos on the Grill's parking lot than running the Grill. But when he acquired the property in 2005, he knew that keeping the beloved Grill open was important for the community. He did open a twenty-six-unit condominium complex adjacent to the Grill and named it The Lacey after his predecessors.

The Grill's origin in 1944 actually predates the term "soul food," which emerged in the 1960s. To the average American, soul food is known as food traditionally eaten in the African-American community. But it's not that simple. According to soul food historian Adrian Miller, "soul food" is traced to the Deep South's slavery era. In rural areas before the Civil War, the slave diet was mainly vegan, relying heavily on beans and vegetables like cabbage, okra, and watercress. Biscuits, fried chicken, and catfish were not readily accessible and were reserved for special occasions. But after Emancipation, when black Americans migrated north and to cities, these special-occasion foods were more readily available and no longer saved solely for special occasions. And so the idea of soul food narrowed to these fatty foods that had previously been infrequent entrees. Poet and essayist Amiri Baraka is credited with coining the phrase "soul food" in his 1960s book *Home: Social Essays*.

During the civil rights movement, the word "soul" came into vogue as a way to celebrate black culture. Soul food had been around for decades, but the term was essentially a marketing tool to celebrate black cuisine. "Soul music," "soul sister," and "soul brother" all popped up in the American lexicon.

"Soul food" conjures some negative connotations within the black community. Some people think that slaves were given the leftovers from their masters and dislike the idea of celebrating cuisine that continues this tradition of inequality. Diabetes is also more common among black Americans than whites, and many blame the modern soul food diet.

Unlike cuisines of other minority groups, soul food has not really transcended its own community. Mexican, Chinese, Indian, and Italian dishes are prepared in homes of all races. My Irish mother regularly cooked fajitas, chicken teriyaki, and lasagna for dinner, but never chitterlings or candied yams. Part of this was that we lived in New Jersey, but part of it is that these soul food items have yet to truly transcend southern or black kitchens.

One exception is macaroni and cheese. A comfort food in all fifty states, mac and cheese is no longer a food for the sick, black, southern, or juvenile. Upscale restaurants have embraced "grown-up" macaroni and cheese in recent years, infusing the classic dish with gourmet flairs like multiple cheese combinations, meat, lobster, and seasonings.

For a more in-depth look at the history of soul food, pick up a copy of Adrian Miller's book *Soul Food: The Surprising Story of an American Cuisine, One Plate at a Time* from the Grill's counter. Along with Tracye McQuirter's vegan health guide *By Any Greens Necessary* for black women, it's there for any customer to browse and return.

Both books will suggest you avoid eating fried chicken and buttery biscuits for every meal. But as with most things in life, moderation is key. Soul food may not be the healthiest cuisine to eat 24/7, but every now and then, it's okay to indulge. And when you do, perch yourself on a stool at the Florida Avenue Grill.

FROZEN DAIRY BAR EATERY

6641 ARLINGTON BOULEVARD • FALLS CHURCH, VA 22042

(703) 534-4200 • FDBPIZZA.COM

History on Ice

In the last two years, six frozen yogurt shops opened within a mile and a half of the Frozen Dairy Bar. But a lineup of new competitors made only a dent in business. Sweet tooths have been satisfied here since 1950, where frozen custard reigns supreme. Inspired by the summertime pleasures of enjoying a cold treat at the beach, the addition of pizza to the menu brings the ocean's greatest boardwalk indulgences inland.

LeRoy Eakin relocated from Kansas to the DC area in the 1920s. Eakin saw opportunity growing in the farmlands that dominated the Falls Church area. He purchased some of that land and launched a career in commercial real estate. On land owned by Eakin, Guy and Walter Sponseller opened the Frozen Dairy Bar (FDB) in 1950. LeRoy's wife, Ruth P. Eakin, one of the first women to graduate from Harvard's architectural school, designed the building. A six-foot-tall vanilla cone stood on top of the roadside stand. At night, electricity surged through the cone and rooftop lettering. The bright white cone and red letters beckoned custard-craving patrons inside.

The current incarnation of the Frozen Dairy Bar offers many flavors, but the original offered just the classics: chocolate and vanilla. And for the last sixty-five years, vanilla has held the crown for most ordered flavor, on par with national trends. (This chocoholic was surprised to learn that vanilla outsells chocolate two to one across the country.)

"Frozen custard is something you don't see very often," says Kevin Eakin, managing partner of the firm that owns FDB. "A lot of people don't really understand what it is."

Let me break it down: frozen custard is softer, warmer, and denser than ice cream. The churning process for both ice cream and custard incorporates air, but frozen custard ends up containing less air. "It has a lot more of what makes ice cream *ice cream*," says Mike Natoli, FDB's general manager and head chef. With less air than ice cream, frozen custard has a richer flavor. Frozen custard is also stored at a higher temperature than ice cream. Ice cream is traditionally stored at ten degrees, while frozen custard is stored at between twenty and twenty-six degrees. To be considered frozen custard, a product must have at least 10 percent butterfat. Ice cream may include no butterfat. "Our scoops are a little smaller because you're still getting the same amount of cream as you would [in a larger size]," says Natoli.

Over the years, FDB changed locations a handful of times but has always been tied to the Eakin family. In 2000, LeRoy's son Richard bought FDB. "The owners mentioned they were thinking of selling the business," says Kevin, Richard's son. "[My father] didn't want to see it go away, so he decided to purchase the Frozen Dairy Bar and keep it alive."

The business's survival required a little rebranding. "The thing about ice cream [businesses] here in the Northeast is 90 percent of the sales take place for five months of the year," says Natoli. "You have to be able to sustain yourself the rest of the year." Unlike self-serve frozen yogurt shops that have become very trendy, FDB needs more than one employee to run the place. That puts more pressure to sell in the winter, when most people aren't craving frozen desserts. With ever-increasing development in DC and its suburbs, there has also been more competition than ever before, particularly with branded establishments.

FDB's answer to both challenges? Pizza.

In 2004, FDB simply added pizza to its frozen custard counter, and the establishment became known as the Frozen Dairy Bar and Boardwalk Pizza. Today at FDB, a partition divides a frozen custard counter with a few tables from a sit-down area providing table service. "We've tried to create a separation [between] the frozen custard operation and the pizza so they can coexist without affecting one another," says Natoli.

And they've succeeded. A family can come in for a round of custard cones at the counter and grab a table out of view from a couple enjoying a more adult dinner and vice versa.

"It's a cool niche," says Kevin. Two concepts under one roof "gives us a little something different than all the branded competition in our neighborhood."

Natoli oversees the kitchen, where he and his staff make their pizza dough from scratch. Pizzas range from commonplace Hawaiian and margherita to pesto chicken and Asian duck, which tops fontina and Asiago cheeses with shredded duck, green onions, and hoisin sauce. For celiac haters, there's gluten-free pizza, and for Ben Wyatt enthusiasts, there's calzones.

The frozen custard selection has also expanded well beyond the FDB's original two flavors. For instance, Natoli created taro and mango flavors to appeal to a large Vietnamese population in the area. Everything's made from scratch, from the custard to the waffle bowls and fruit compote. FDB also serves desserts that require a bit more finesse than guiding a swirl into a cone. FDB's take on the Blizzard is affectionately known as "goose bumps," as in, you'll have them when you taste how good it is. The bananas Foster is also popular. This New Orleans dish combines hot bananas glazed in rum and cinnamon with vanilla frozen custard, candied pecans, and whipped cream.

Kevin says the future looks bright for the Frozen Dairy Bar, fresh off the heels of its expansion. "We want everyone who comes in to come back again."

Many do. Just last year, a couple came in to celebrate their fiftieth wedding anniversary. Their love story began half a century earlier with a first date at the Frozen Dairy Bar. Fifty years from now, perhaps a couple will come in for a slice of pizza to celebrate the pie that started it all.

Eighteenth-Century Eats

When you hear the word "skyscraper," you probably think of the Empire State Building, Sears Tower, or Demi Lovato. You probably *don't* think of a four-story brick building. But in the late 1700s, the people of Alexandria did. In 1792, Gadsby's Tavern, the focal point of Alexandria's social life, became the tallest structure in the city.

Originally called City Tavern, the restaurant opened in 1785 under John Wise. According to Gadsby's Tavern museum director Gretchen Bulova, Alexandria was a thriving seaport at the time. With plans for the nation's capital to move from Philadelphia to a newly created city of Washington, DC, travelers would need somewhere to refuel and rest. Wise wanted City Tavern to meet that demand. Washington, DC, was officially founded on July 16, 1790, and included Alexandria. In 1792, Wise built the skyscraping addition that contained fourteen rooms to provide respite for our nation's earliest government employees. By 1800, DC officially became our capital, and in 1846, Alexandria was given the boot: it returned to the domain of Virginia.

In 1796, Wise turned the tavern over to John Gadsby, who really "put this place on the map," says Bulova. Gadsby was savvy enough to start his own stagecoach lines between Alexandria and Georgetown and Baltimore that necessitated a stay at his inn. Under his leadership, Gadsby's Tavern became well known along the East Coast, and Gadsby himself became synonymous with hospitality. Bulova says Thomas Jefferson even called Gadsby a "credit to his industry."

Gadsby's Tavern was not just a pit stop for travelers. It was a setting for America's early political development. It was at Gadsby's that George Mason wrote the Fairfax Resolves, which rejected British sovereignty over the colonies, an early step in the Revolutionary War.

Gadsby's was also the center of Alexandria's social world. Elegant dances took place in its ballrooms. Gadsby's honored George Washington with two Birthnight Balls in 1797 and 1798. The name jabbed at our former monarchs: Birthnight Balls in Great Britain honored the king, but newly independent, we threw our own Birthnight Balls for Washington. Washington was unable to attend the ball in 1797 due to presidential duties in Philadelphia, but he attended the following year, after John Adams had succeeded him.

Many of our nation's original VIPs ate and drank at Gadsby's, including George Washington, Thomas Jefferson, John Adams, James Madison, Ben Franklin, Francis Scott Key, James Monroe, Aaron Burr, and Henry Clay.

The colonial charm and elegance these men enjoyed remains for today's visitors. "What you see here is our best attempt at keeping it the way it was," says assistant general manager Alan White while sporting breeches and a puffy white shirt. White's shirt looks an awful lot like *Seinfeld*'s "puffy shirt," but it looks more at home among the old wooden tables and candles than Jerry did in the modern world.

On the walls hang various paintings and prints, including a 1798 city plan for Alexandria and a print of *Washington at the Battle of Trenton*. Take a look at two particularly fun prints from English painter and satirist William Hogarth: *Beer Street* and *Gin Lane*. These propagandist prints discouraged London's poor from drinking too much gin and creating general mayhem in the streets. On *Gin Lane*, a baby falls out of its exposed mother's arms and buildings in the background crumble. On *Beer Lane*, however, fully clothed, respectable commoners socialize in front of sturdy buildings. A large painting by Hogarth also hangs in the main dining room. It depicts several men drinking rum punch, a popular concoction of the period.

The menu features hearty meats and fish that our founding fathers enjoyed. Meat loaf, ale-battered crispy cod, crab cakes, and veal cutlet are just a few of the items on the menu, which includes "George Washington's Favorite," a grilled breast of duck with scalloped potatoes, corn pudding, rhotekraut, and port wine orange glacé. The lunch entrees are very reasonably priced; the ale-braised duck sausage will only set you back $13.

In 1926, the American Legion's Alexandria chapter purchased and restored Gadsby's Tavern and continues to operate it today. Gadsby's became a national landmark in 1964. "Any major changes, we have to go through the city first," explains White. The fireplaces also remain unlit. Burning down a national landmark is not on the agenda.

But dancing is. Each year, Gadsby's re-creates George Washington's birthday bash, and every four years, the inn restages Jefferson's inaugural ball. Everyone's in costume, of course.

Gadsby's also sponsors several food and beverage programs, such as the annual rum punch challenge. Participants build on sponsor Bacardi's rum with their own recipes to celebrate the punch so popular during the inn's early days. Gadsby's also hosts a Madeira tasting every Presidents' Day weekend. "This was *the* drink for the founding fathers," says Bulova. "You can imagine them all reclining with a book and a glass of Madeira."

On Friday and Saturday nights, historian John Douglass Hall interacts with patrons as a typical colonist and might play the lute guitar if you ask nicely. Hall also travels the country as a James Madison impersonator. "If his wife didn't make him, he wouldn't have electricity at his house," says White.

Before you leave, be sure to peek around the corner for a look at Gadsby's old ice well. Gadsby stocked ice not only for his tavern but to sell to the public as well.

It may not be a skyscraper, but Gadsby's Tavern aims high to give visitors a taste of what life was like for our founding fathers around the table and on the dance floor.

IDLE TIME BOOKS

2467 18TH STREET NW • WASHINGTON, DC 20009

(202) 232-4774 • IDLETIMEBOOKS.COM

Book Lovers

Valerie and Jacques Morgan loved books, but not the same kind of books.

"We'd sit up in bed and look at what each other was reading and go, 'Oh God!'" Val recalls of her late husband. Jacques preferred science fiction, mystery novels, and anything about popular culture. Val prefers travel writing and memoirs. Together they opened Idle Time Books, a used and rare books store, in 1981.

Val and Jacques met in 1977. A New Zealand native traveling the globe, she was just passing through DC. She spent a month getting to know Jacques and then continued on her travels. But her attraction to Jacques pulled her back to DC in 1980.

An avid book collector, Jacques had "books everywhere," Val says. She suggested they open a bookstore. And so, in 1981, they started Idle Time Books. "It was a rinky-dink little affair," Val reflects. But they paid the bills. With $100,000 they got from auctioning off Jacques's extensive comic book collection, they bought the three-story brick building the bookstore now occupies.

The duo divided their duties: Val handled the administrative work, and Jacques stuck to sourcing and pricing books. As they got older, they agreed that Jacques should avoid working the register. "He would get really grumpy," Val laughs. "In the old days—I'm talking thirty, forty years ago—all old used-book stores were owned by old people. You walked in the door

[and] you didn't bother them," says Val. But as businesses have become more service-oriented, customers would ask for suggestions. "[He'd think] 'I don't know you! I don't know what you want to read!'" recalls Val. "He'd be sourcing a book and someone would want to buy a greeting card with a credit card. . . . We found it better not to let him behind the counter too much." But for serious book collectors like himself, Jacques rolled out the charm.

Located on 18th Street in Adams Morgan, Idle Time Books has become a destination for book lovers in search of the old but good. Section titles are written on pieces of paper in Sharpie. There is no thematic decor. In a small section on pregnancy and parenting, a few cut-out portraits of babies dressed as celebrities hang on the wall. In the African-American history section, a round bumper sticker from the March on Washington hangs next to a scattered collection of protest photos. A sign playing on Barack Obama's campaign slogan affirms "YES WE CAN put books back where we found them."

Books line each step leading to the second and third floors. The second floor is more of a half floor, a brief pit stop with just a few shelves. The third floor boasts an impressive political section. The section dividers are vast and specific: the Pentagon Papers, Presidential Papers, Globalization, NATO, Disarmament, Elections, and biographies in alphabetical order.

The U.S. history section also features many subdivisions, from the Early American Republic to the Civil War and Reconstruction, in addition to titles arranged by region and state.

"As you go deeper into the store, you go deeper into the categories," explains Val. She says you have to have all sorts of categories, some ultra-specific. Customers will cry, "'What do you mean you don't have any sewing books?!'" Val laughs. Most customers come in looking for fiction, and philosophy is also very popular.

"Some people are flummoxed," says Val. "[They think] 'Where the hell am I? I've walked into a museum.'" But many are overjoyed to find a shop

Vintage Spot
Dan's Café

This Adams Morgan dive bar has been (barely) serving drinks since 1965. If you want a drink, you'll have to mix it yourself. Liquor comes in a squeeze bottle with a bucket of ice and a mixer for you to do what you wish. There's no AC in the summer, and it's cash-only. If you're looking for a place to drink with zero frills, this is it.

2315 18th Street NW, Washington, DC 20009 (202) 265-0299

with a sole proprietor that has survived in a neighborhood that has changed so much in the last three decades. "The rents have gone up," says Val. When she and Jacques first moved into Adams Morgan, the neighborhood had much more retail than it does now. But restaurants and bars have replaced the clothing stores, furniture repair shops, and other retail stores that once dominated the neighborhood. In the age of Barnes and Noble, some customers aren't used to coming into a small bookstore. And in an age of Nooks and Kindles, fewer book collectors are on the hunt to add to their libraries.

The Adams Morgan neighborhood got its name by combining the names of the John Quincy Adams School for white students and the Thomas P. Morgan School for black students. When DC integrated its schools in 1955, the principals of the schools created the Adams-Morgan Better Neighborhood Conference to promote a peaceful, integrated community. The name stuck. Known for being artsy and diverse, Adams Morgan befits its origin story.

Val and Jacques lived a modest life. They shopped at thrift stores and valued fulfillment over money. "We didn't need to make a lot of money, and that was why we stayed in business," Val says. It was about the books.

Jacques died in 2012. Val has assumed his duties. "Jacques was always on the hunt for books. I'm trying to keep that game up," she says. And sorting through Jacques's "basement of treasures" is a task that's still not complete.

Val plans to continue working for the next few years and then assess what the future holds. "When your spouse dies on you, you start feeling your mortality," she says. But for now, the sixty-four-year-old can run up and down three flights of stairs every day without issue. Her secret to success is "the love of it." And that love for a business she and Jacques built together has yet to fade.

IRON GATE

1734 N STREET NW • WASHINGTON, DC 20036
(202) 524-5202 • IRONGATERESTAURANTDC.COM

Supper in the Stables

GTV and the History Channel would have a field day with the Iron Gate Restaurant. With owners on opposing sides of history and stables that were converted into a refined restaurant, the Iron Gate is a designer and historian's match made in heaven.

You enter the Iron Gate through—you guessed it—an iron gate. The entryway is tucked into an alley between Dupont Circle town houses. A row of lanterns leading to the doorway establishes a theme that continues throughout the establishment.

The Iron Gate is divided into three separate areas: the bar, the garden, and the restaurant. All are open year-round. The bar and garden offer a casual, aesthetic spot to munch on affordable plates, while the restaurant offers pricey four- and six-course tasting menus.

Executive chef and co-owner Anthony Chittum explains, "I want to offer a less expensive, casual feel for people, and [that] fits the patio and bar." However, he counters, "I want to get fancy sometimes." That's what the tasting menu provides. The Iron Gate's setup "gives me the opportunity to do both."

The Iron Gate's romantic atmosphere originates from Chittum's own romance. He married a Greek woman, and when traveling to visit her family, Greece's outdoor dining spaces and unique converted architecture stuck with him. Chittum recalls visiting a restaurant in Greece built where a structure burned down. The only remnants of the former building were its frame of bricks. The restaurant turned that space into its garden, bricks and all.

Although the majority of Chittum's culinary training focused on modern American, French, and Italian food, he noticed the overlaps between Greek and mid-Atlantic cuisines, namely the abundance of seafood and the seasonality of food. The transition into preparing Greek dishes was seamless.

The entryway opens into the bar. A long, narrow space, it once served as the house's carriageway. It now holds six tables and a long bar that comfortably seats about fifteen.

Outside, a patio and garden sit under latticework entangled with small lanterns and wisteria. Couches flank fire pits in the winter, and potted plants grow on a wooden fence.

Off the patio, the former stables of the property now house the restaurant. Dimly lit, the romantic atmosphere is enhanced by red booths, low ceilings, and a pairing of brick and wooden walls.

The house was built in 1875 and has had two prominent, contradictory owners: the first is Nelson Appleton Miles, a Union soldier in the Civil War and a leading general in the Great Plains Wars against Native Americans. His military success in the 1870s and 1880s forced many Native Americans onto reservations. Miles was also an important figure in the Spanish-American War. As commanding general of the U.S. Army, he led the American invasion of Puerto Rico in 1898, which ultimately yielded its annexation. At the age of seventy-seven, Miles volunteered to serve in World War I but was politely turned away. He died eight years later in 1925 and is buried in Arlington National Cemetery.

Miles sold his estate in 1908 to a couple from New York, and in 1922, they sold it to the General Federation of Women's Clubs (GFWC) for use as their national headquarters. Founded in 1890, the GFWC is a service institution that improved child labor laws, helped pass the Pure Food and Drug Act, and created hundreds of public libraries. In 1921, the GFWC created the Indian Welfare Committee to preserve Native American culture

Vintage Spot

mama ayesha's

After working as a cook at the Syrian Embassy, Jerusalem-born farmer Ayesha Abraham opened this Middle Eastern restaurant in 1960. She named it Calvert Café, but after her death in 1993, Abraham's family renamed the restaurant in her honor. They continue to run it today, serving authentic Middle Eastern dishes like *mujaddara* and *makloubeh*.

**1967 Calvert Street NW, Washington, DC 20009,
(202) 232-5431, mamaayeshas.com**

and improve health, education, and daily life on reservations—the same reservations that their command center's former owner worked to populate.

In 1923, the GFWC converted General Miles's stables into a tearoom for members and nonmembers to enjoy. During Prohibition, tearooms were all the rage, functioning as the female equivalent of a saloon.

In 1928, the GFWC turned the tearoom over to Marie Mount, who converted the space into a restaurant, the first Iron Gate Inn. The restaurant kept its name under several owners. In 1957, Charles Saah adapted the Iron Gate into a Middle Eastern restaurant, and in 1991, Nabeel David converted it into a Mediterranean restaurant. David operated the Iron Gate until 2010, when the Iron Gate closed its doors for three years.

Then, in 2013, the Neighborhood Restaurant Group (NRG) partnered with Chittum to reopen the Iron Gate. "We came in at the right time to give it a new lease on life," says NRG public relations director Megan Bailey. NRG's "chef-driven culture" supported Chittum's reimagining of the Iron Gate with dual Mediterranean menus, according to Bailey.

Small plates to share, large plates for one, and four- or six-course tasting menus showcase Chittum's mastery of cuisine. From small plates like pork kalamaki with yogurt sauce and grilled lemon to whole plates like kale salad with pickled egg, rotisserie chicken, and pecorino vinaigrette, the plates are varied and affordable. My favorite is the delicious spinach-ricotta cannelloni topped with garlic bread crumbs.

The tasting menu promises a wide variety of dishes, beginning with a seasonal sharing plate and then progressing to vegetable, fish, meat, cheese, and dessert courses. Sixty dollars gets you four courses, and $80 gets you six.

The Iron Gate's dual menus bring a range of guests through the doors. "Two menus appeal to different people, and also the same people at different times," says Megan Bailey. Whether you're looking to enjoy affordable small plates or drop more money on a special occasion, Chittum has a menu for you.

The Iron Gate has a long history, and Chittum plans to extend it. While the overwhelming majority of restaurants fail in the first one to three years, Chittum says, "I want to retire from this restaurant." Lucky for you, that's a long ways away.

JOE'S RECORD PARADISE

8216 GEORGIA AVENUE • SILVER SPRING, MD 20910

(301) 585-3269 • JOESRECORDPARADISE.COM

Don't throw the past away
You might need it some rainy day
Dreams can come true again
When everything old is new again

S o sings Peter Allen. And he's right. The past resurfaces in the future, from fashion to technology. That's why overalls are trendy again and vinyl sales are way up.

Americans purchased 9.2 million vinyl records in 2014, a 52 percent increase from 2013. Vinyl sales were huge in the 1970s and 1980s, but when CDs took over in the 1990s, they plummeted. Digital downloads replaced CDs, but vinyl has made a comeback. Although 2014's vinyl sales were dismal compared to vinyl's glory days three decades ago, steady increases in the last few years suggest that the trend will only continue.

Johnson Lee, owner of Joe's Record Paradise, agrees: "People are just hip to the format again." Lee predicts, "In the next ten years, we're going to see so many record collections flood the market."

As baby boomers sell their collections, those records may end up at Joe's Record Paradise. Although the store has changed locations a few times, its commitment to serving DC's music needs has remained constant since 1974.

The store is divided into two rooms. Music lovers enter through the first, smaller room, which contains an impressive collection of random music, books, and VHS tapes, along with a bizarre shrine to local musician Root Boy Slim that includes a pair of Root Boy's boxers and a Barbie doll. The room smells like the incense burning from the register. The scent disappears as you enter the much larger, second room.

This room's walls are pink, the carpet's purple, and the crates are full. Records play over the PA. Customers browse while the sweet crackle of the record player resounds in between songs. Used and new records, CDs, and 45s are stacked by genre. Most records are priced at $6.50, and the selection is so vast that international buyers sometimes come to Paradise to stock their own stores abroad.

Posters of bands and album covers from the Rolling Stones, Aretha Franklin, Pink Floyd, Marvin Gaye, and the Sex Pistols are just a few of the things that litter the walls. Random objects like a bust of Elvis wearing a sparkly gold hat and a movie still of Glenn Close can be found throughout the store. Worn-out copies of *Alternative Press* and *Musik* sit on a shelf in the corner. It's slightly grungy. But that's part of the appeal. The focus is the music.

Joe Lee opened Joe's Record Paradise in 1974. He was well connected to local musicians and radio stations, particularly WHFS. In fact, Joe Lee was instrumental in keeping one of the station's DJs employed.

According to Johnson, WHFS "would play rock and roll that no one else would play." The station "wasn't corporate." But corporate was exactly where new owner Duchossois Communications wanted to take things in 1989. Beloved DJ Damian Einstein had a speech impediment that resulted from a car accident. He was "promoted" off-air to a nonspeaking position. Joe Lee organized a "Save Damian" rally that drew ten thousand supporters to Joe's. The next year, Damian was back on the air.

After working as a DJ playing mostly house music, Johnson started working for his father and took over Joe's Record Paradise about five years ago. It was a relatively easy transition. "I was raised at the store basically," Johnson says. Johnson was responsible for scouting the store's current Silver Spring location; he laid the carpet and painted the walls himself. Like his father, Johnson promotes local talent by organizing free concerts at the store every few months.

About 1,400 independent record stores currently operate in the nation. Since 2007, many have participated in Record Store Day. On the third Saturday of every April, artists perform at these stores and release limited records. "It's a good day for us as far as the numbers go," says Johnson. Many consumers opt for deals online rather than purchase from actual stores, but "it does bring attention to vinyl," Johnson commends.

And it's not just old records. Today's artists even know that vinyl achieves a unique sound that enriches the listening experience. Taylor Swift's album *Red* is available on vinyl, and *The Lego Movie* released its soundtrack on vinyl. What was old is new again.

Much has been written about our shortening attention spans and inability to focus on one thing at a time. We have cars that can read our text messages, computers that double as televisions, and our phones contain more technology than our first spaceships did. But a record player does one thing: plays the record. That singularity is appealingly simple.

So too is a record itself. It's big. It's tangible. It's something you can collect. Flipping through a crate of records feels a whole lot more satisfying than scrolling down a never-ending page on Amazon. A vinyl collection has mass; an iTunes playlist does not.

Johnson Lee has two children he could pass Joe's Record Paradise down to, but they're seven and three. Will Joe's still be around for them to run twenty years from now? "If we're lucky," says Johnson. If the store could survive the domination of CDs in the 1990s and the age of digital downloads, I'd bet on Joe's.

KRAMERBOOKS &

AFTERWORDS CAFÉ

1517 CONNECTICUT AVENUE NW • WASHINGTON, DC 20036

(202) 387-1400 • KRAMERS.COM

The Right to Read

There's something romantic about Kramerbooks. It's the kind of intimate bookstore where a girl who loves poetry and a boy who's shopping for his mother's birthday present would "meet cute" in a romantic comedy. Nora Ephron and Mindy Kaling would love it.

This Dupont Circle literary haven combines books with a full-service restaurant and bar and can brag that it's the nation's very first bookstore/cafe combo. Every time you step into a big chain bookstore and order a cappuccino while perusing a book you have no plans to buy, you have Kramerbooks to thank.

Since opening in 1976, Kramerbooks has become the kind of "hidden gem" that everybody knows about, while somehow maintaining its sense of low-key cool. The space is oddly shaped, and the shelves don't rise beyond three feet or so. Consequently, you can always see the other shoppers. There's no hiding in an aisle with a copy of Jason Priestley's memoir. Your book selections are for public consumption. But there's something great about that. Without contained aisles, you feel wonderfully and completely surrounded by literature.

The bookstore hosts readings by authors and music performances ranging from jazz and folk to country and blues.

The book selection is varied. A small children's section joins adult books ranging from best sellers like *The Casual Vacancy* to *How to Tell If Your Cat Is Plotting to Kill You.* A box of psychology games and Mr. and Mrs. Obama paper dolls also grace the shelves.

Kramerbooks' clientele is diverse. You are likely to see students, senior citizens, young parents, and people of all races browsing the book selection and dining at the Afterwords Café. It's not just a coffee and pastry cart; it's a full-service restaurant serving breakfast, lunch, dinner, and brunch. The bar is open twenty-four hours on weekends and until 1 a.m. on weekdays. The dinner menu features tacos, a crab cake pasta, Jamaican curried goat, and butternut squash ravioli, to name a few of the entrees that hover around $18. The brunch menu includes banana-stuffed french toast and a trout and salmon fish platter, along with plenty of burgers, omelets, and breakfast fare.

If you find yourself filled with the sense that your First Amendment rights are safe and sound at Kramerbooks, it's because the bookstore was at the center of a national discussion about freedom of speech in the late 1990s.

As part of his investigation into Bill Clinton's indiscretions with Monica Lewinsky, a judge subpoenaed Kramerbooks for a list of the purchases that Lewinsky made there. "I received the subpoena," says co-owner David Tenney. "I laughed. I cried. I called our lawyer."

In a deposition, Clinton had said that Lewinsky gave him "a book or two," and Lewinsky had told Linda Tripp that she gave Clinton the 1992 phone sex novel *Vox* by Nicholson Baker as a gift. The subpoena on Kramerbooks (and Georgetown's Barnes and Noble) was part of the effort to corroborate this information. When the American Civil Liberties Union (ACLU) misheard that Kramerbooks had complied with the subpoena, they picketed the store.

"We did not like being picketed by the ACLU," says Tenney. "We hired a PR firm and said, 'No, we are not going to give up the goods.'" The ACLU was satisfied, but Kramerbooks still had to deal with prosecutor Kenneth Starr. They planned to appeal. But before doing so, all parties reached a settlement: Lewinsky agreed to give Starr her list of purchases.

Kramerbooks was satisfied with the outcome, having accomplished what they intended: to protect their customers' privacy. The bookstore also avoided additional legal costs, which had already tallied into six figures. Luckily, the American Booksellers Association picked up the tab.

The First Amendment issue resonated strongly with DC and the nation, as about a decade earlier, *City Paper* had printed a list of the videos that conservative Supreme Court nominee Robert H. Bork rented while he was being considered for the bench. He was ultimately not confirmed.

Tenney saw the silver lining of the situation: The bookstore received a lot of good press for sticking it to the man, and "we got a snappy T-shirt [out of it]." Kramerbooks printed up black T-shirts with "Subpoenaed For Bookselling" lettered in gold.

Kramerbooks has avoided the political spotlight since Y2K but has remained a fixture in the community. "The purpose was always to confront middle-class values, to be proud of our ability to shape reading tastes, to respect each other, and to have fun. Possibly in that order," says Tenney. The easiest part of that goal to verify on paper—financial success—seems to be alive and well. Every time I've been to Kramerbooks, it's been full of customers.

In 2011, President Obama was one of those patrons. He visited Kramer's with his daughters, Sasha and Malia, on Small Business Saturday. He did not purchase the Mr. and Mrs. Obama paper dolls, opting instead for a copy of *Descent into Chaos: The U.S. and the Disaster in Pakistan, Afghanistan, and Central Asia.*

Kramerbooks has survived for forty years, but Tenney's not giving up any insider info as to why. "I'm not telling our secrets, and I'll be dead in forty years." Even if *he's* in the ground four decades from now, I don't think Kramerbooks will be.

Tex-Mex with a Side of the American Dream

*L*uis Reyes came to America with $150 sewn into his pocket. In a true rags-to-riches tale, the El Salvadoran immigrant turned that $150 into millions as the owner of the wildly popular restaurant Lauriol Plaza.

In the 1970s, civil war was brewing in El Salvador. Violence and poverty plagued the nation. Too many people had too little. Reyes was one of them. "I come from a very poor background," he says. His childhood home lacked indoor plumbing, and he didn't have a pair of shoes until age seven.

In 1977 at sixteen, Reyes paid a smuggler (aka a "coyote") to get him into the United States. But the coyote left his group in the Mexican desert. They went without food for five days. Eventually Reyes made it across the border and set foot in Washington, DC, by New Year's Day of 1978. It was a fitting date of arrival for the teenager, whose new beginning would prove very fruitful.

For three years, Reyes worked as an undocumented dishwasher and cook. In 1981, he toyed with the idea of returning to El Salvador to fight with the FMLN—the insurgent group that had started a civil war with the government two years earlier. But he knew that returning to the United States would be very difficult, so he decided to stay. He would find another way to help Salvadorans.

It came in the form of Lauriol Plaza. Reyes teamed with restaurateur Raul Sanchez to open the restaurant in 1983. Soon enough, with a successful enterprise on his hands, Reyes joined the many Salvadorans who send

money back to their home country. These remittances account for about 20 percent of the country's gross domestic product.

Like Reyes, Raul Sanchez rose from humble beginnings into a powerful restaurateur. Sanchez grew up in La Havana, Cuba, and immigrated to DC at age twenty-two with $5 in his pocket. He worked as a busboy and then a server at a popular Cuban restaurant. His mother joined him three years later in DC, and together they opened a boardinghouse similar to the one she'd run in Cuba. The business evolved into a food delivery service, which generated enough income for Sanchez to open his first Cuban/Spanish restaurant. After a few years, he sold the restaurant and opened a second that focused on Spanish, Cuban, and Mexican cuisine. He sold this restaurant as well, and the profits enabled him to open Lauriol Plaza and, later, Cactus Cantina, both of which he still owns. A collection of framed pictures depicting Cuban street scenes and people grace the first-floor walls. Framed Cuban currency through the years also hangs on the wall, showing the change in coins and bills from 1902 to 1959.

Lauriol Plaza serves simple, satisfying food of the Tex-Mex and Latin American varieties. The menu reflects its owners' backgrounds, Reyes from El Salvador and Sanchez from Cuba. Items like the chicken quesadilla and the fajitas deliver nothing out of the ordinary but are very popular, as are the seafood dishes. The *camarones brochette* delivers six cheese- and jalapeño-stuffed jumbo shrimp wrapped in bacon to your watering mouth, and the *masitas de puerco*, Cuban-style bites of pork marinated in *criollo* sauce and roasted in Sevilla's bitter oranges, are sure to please. To satisfy an after-dinner sweet tooth, try the *cajeta* ice cream. *Cajeta* is a traditional Mexican syrup made from goat's milk, sugar, and cinnamon. Lauriol Plaza's includes coconut and caramel.

Of course, any good Tex-Mex restaurant wouldn't be complete without a good batch of margaritas and sangria. Lauriol Plaza has both. To start the week off right, the restaurant features Half-Pitcher Margarita Mondays for $16.95. At any time of the day, choose from lime, strawberry, mango, or

Vintage Spot

Cactus Cantina

The sister restaurant to Raul Sanchez and Luis Reyes's Lauriol Plaza, this Tex-Mex restaurant has been open for twenty-five years and served George W. and Laura Bush in 2003. Look for the giant cactus outside that matches the green awning and umbrellas outside the brick building.

3300 Wisconsin Avenue NW, Washington, DC 20016,
(202) 686-7222, cactuscantina.com

peach-flavored pitchers. Lauriol Plaza also offers glasses, pitchers, or half pitchers of its sangria, in addition to mojitos, a cocktail that originated in Cuba.

If you want a table, come in the afternoon. Even with a restaurant so large, patrons sometimes have to wait an hour or two to get in. Outdoor seating under canopies lines the block outside and on a third-floor terrace.

The clientele ranges in age from twenty-five to forty-five and is very diverse. Famous diners have included Bill Clinton, Michelle Obama, and Al Gore. (President George W. Bush preferred Reyes and Sanchez's other restaurant, Cactus Cantina.) DC also has a Salvadoran population of 250,000, and Lauriol Plaza serves as a gathering place for some.

Reyes has used his restaurant as a base for his own political work. In the 2009 Salvadoran election, he campaigned for FMLN candidate Mauricio Funes, who went on to win the election and served as El Salvador's president until 2014.

The restaurant is enormous, with very high ceilings and plenty of room for steam to rise from sizzling fajitas. A gigantic seasonal mural serves as the one major work of art. It changes four times a year with the weather. On a winter afternoon, the mural showcases an ice-skating scene.

This is Lauriol Plaza's second location. After their former lease expired, Reyes and Sanchez decided to build a new space instead of renting, a relatively uncommon approach in the city. They constructed the gigantic, three-floor space that now holds Lauriol Plaza.

From dishwasher to owner, Reyes has truly embodied and achieved the American Dream. "There is not a country in the world like the United States. This country is amazing," he remarks. The dual citizen has lived in DC much longer than he lived in El Salvador. The place where he lives, works, and helps others, "This is my home."

Italian Aisles

*T*his is the best olive oil ever," a young woman tries to convince her grandmother. She's clutching a $6 bottle, one of more than eighty varieties packing the shelves of A. Litteri, a small grocery store with authentic Italian wares.

Brothers Mariano DeFrancisci and Antonio Litteri immigrated to the United States from Palermo, Sicily, in the early 1920s. They decided to capitalize on their knowledge of Italian goods. In 1926, they opened A. Litteri. DeFrancisci's great-nephew owns and runs the store today.

Unless you know where to look, you're unlikely to find this treasure trove of Italian products just outside of Gallaudet University's campus. It's tucked away on a side street off 6th that looks like a row of warehouses. But an entrance painted green and red for the Italian flag separates A. Litteri from the less-inviting warehouses on its sides.

Inside, narrow, jam-packed shelves showcase all the essential trappings of Italian cuisine. The dozens of olive oils lining one aisle are a beautiful sight to behold for this Italian writer. For hard-core olive oil enthusiasts, A. Litteri even sells olive oil soaps. Also, jars and jars of plain olives.

An aisle of thirty types of balsamic vinegars also impresses. The store features a plethora of balsamic flavors: raspberry, cranberry, fig, and pomegranate, to name a few.

Rows of wine organized by country of origin take over a corner of the store. Italian wine is "the best wine in the world," says Ken Nankervis, A.

Litteri's wine specialist and store manager. After three decade in the wine and hospitality industries, he should know. According to Nankervis, because Italy grows 1,300 types of grapes in its twenty-one unique regions, many diverse wines hail from the boot-shaped country. In addition to Italian wines, A. Litteri carries wines from different parts of the United States, plus wines from countries like Australia, New Zealand, South Africa, Germany, and Chile. The Italian wines at A. Litteri sell the best. Customers often come to the store in search of a wine they have read about or enjoyed sipping in Italy.

A. Litteri's dessert section goes well beyond the traditional almond biscotti your local chain grocery store might carry. A. Litteri's biscotti selection includes flavors such as chocolate mint, banana bread, cranberry pistachio, and cinnamon. Other classic Italian sweets like flag/rainbow cookies (my Italian dessert of choice), tiramisu-flavored Piroulines, classic Tuscan cookies, and La Florentine Panettones (the classic Milanese treat made with flour, candy, and raisins) are waiting to be scooped up.

And the pasta ventures far beyond spaghetti. Linguini, ravioli, tortellini, penne, wagon wheels, fusilli, bow ties, rigatoni, tagliatelle, gemelli, elbows, tubetti, and gnocchi line the walls. And there's not just one kind of gnocchi. There's mini, whole wheat, tricolor, cheese. . . . Ravioli gets the same treatment. A freezer stores various types of ravioli and meatballs. A. Litteri stocks all these goodies after buying from local suppliers that import from Italy.

A deli in the back serves up three- and six-foot subs, in addition to orders of meats and cheese. The deli accounts for most of A. Litteri's business. The homemade sausage is also a customer favorite.

Until 1988, A. Litteri sold only wholesale to other providers. But before the decade expired, the store expanded into retail, which now accounts for the business's total trade. Generations of families shop at A. Litteri. "It's a rallying point," says Nankervis of the groups that come in together to get the ingredients they'll need for family dinners.

The neighborhood has a rich history that has changed over the years. During the Civil War, the Union army used Gallaudet's campus as a hospital. In 1968, Pennsylvanian troops called in after the riots to help quell the violence boarded at Gallaudet. In the years afterward, the neighborhood was not so inviting. But as young professionals filled up the neighborhood and crime dropped, the neighborhood improved (and rents skyrocketed). With Gallaudet University and Union Market up the street, more and more people are spending money in the area. Gallaudet also has plans to build a creative and cultural district along 6th Street, infusing the area with even more capital.

Some might argue that the addition of Union Market a few blocks from A. Litteri is good for the Italian bodega's business, but Nankervis sees it the other way around. "If it wasn't for us, they would've never done what they did."

For the new faces in the neighborhood, A. Litteri is confident that a family-run, century-old business has appeal for shoppers interested in the neighborhood's heritage. And great Italian food, of course.

THE MAD HATTER

1319 CONNECTICUT AVENUE NW • WASHINGTON, DC 20036

(202) 833-1495 • MADHATTERDC.COM

We're All Mad Here

Today's most dangerous jobs are in fields like the armed forces, fishing, logging, and construction. But in the 1800s, English hatmakers were living on the edge. These hatmakers used mercury to make and clean their work. After repeatedly breathing in mercury fumes for years, they gradually went mad and became known as "mad hatters." *Alice in Wonderland* features a character known as the Mad Hatter, and he is the inspiration for one of Dupont Circle's favorite bars, the Mad Hatter.

"We were all children of the '60s," says Mickey Tobin of himself and his business partners, Dick Heisenberger and Jack Million. "*Alice in Wonderland,* Lewis Carroll, mushrooms, and all this other stuff . . . we thought it was kind of cute for lack of a better term," Tobin says of choosing a concept for their restaurant and bar.

Alice in Wonderland allusions decorate this DC establishment. The 1865 fantasy nonsense novel by British author Lewis Carroll details the absurd adventures of a young girl named Alice. After falling down a rabbit hole, she meets many strange animals and people, most prominently the Cheshire Cat, the Queen of Hearts, the March Hare, and the Mad Hatter.

The Mad Hatter's first floor is divided into two sections: a bar and a dining room. The dining room boasts high arched ceilings and red walls bearing huge framed prints from *Alice in Wonderland*. Framed movie posters of various *Alice* film incarnations hang in booths toward the back of the dining

room. A four-foot-tall papier-mâché hat perches above the entrance to this half of the joint, putting the hat into Hatter.

The entrance to the bar features a large teacup decorated with hearts, diamonds, and spades, a nod to both the tea party and the card characters in *Alice in Wonderland*.

Graphic designer Lauren Houston curated the entire restaurant and made the Upside Down Room with her own two hands. A small room off the bar, this room features a table on the ceiling set for afternoon tea with cold cuts, fruit, cheese, and sandwiches filling its plates. "She hand painted the ceiling like the Sistine Chapel," says Tobin of the ceiling painted like a black-and-white checkerboard. The paintings in this room also hang upside down, as well as a diagram titled "Eleven Steps in the Making of Men's Hats," but the TV and your reflection in the mirror remain right side up. In *Alice in Wonderland*, Time punished the Mad Hatter and the March Hare by stopping time at 6:00, trapping them in a never-ending teatime party with never-ending trifling conversation. But in this tearoom you can leave anytime you want.

Think twice before writing *Alice* off as pure nonsense. In addition to publishing many works of fiction, Lewis Carroll was an accomplished mathematician who taught math at Oxford and published works on algebra and logic. The teatime scene plays with the "new math" that had emerged in the 1800s. Irish mathematician William Hamilton developed a new number system of "quaternions" that didn't count things, but rather counted rotations. When dealing with tallying rotations, you need to incorporate Time. But Time does not attend the tea party in *Alice in Wonderland*, and the clock's hands cannot rotate. No quaternions means time has stopped, and it's teatime forever.

Tobin, Heisenberger, and Million opened the Mad Hatter in 1981 on M Street. In 2010, native Washingtonians Tobin and Heisenberger moved into the current space, a much larger property. (Million moved to Germany and no longer runs the business with his former partners.) The old Mad Hatter was in the basement of a town house and was about a third of the current establishment's size. "It's been a pretty smooth transition," reflects Tobin. "A lot of the old customers followed us."

At lunchtime, businessmen and women fill the dining room. The happy hour crowd ranges in age from twenty-five to fifty and grows increasingly younger into the night. With more and more young professionals moving into DC, twenty- and thirtysomethings are taking over DC's nightlife. "The city's being New Yorkified, as I like to say," Tobin declares.

Many of those young people end up at the Mad Hatter on weekend nights. Upstairs, the joint feels frattier than downstairs and offers additional seating options at black loveseats, booths, and high tables. On nice days and nights, take advantage of patio seating in the back.

The menu features on-theme items like the Cheshire Nachos, the Hatter Salad, and Alice's Wonder Basket of sliders, chicken fingers, and fries. "People really like our burgers," reports Tobin, who also says that the Cajun Chicken Pasta, a $15 spicy entree in white wine and garlic, is a top seller. "We're basically trying to create a classic American saloon with good food," says Tobin. The Mad Hatter also has a brunch menu featuring staples like chicken and waffles, a steak-and-egg burrito, and even a "Hangover Helper" that comes with biscuits, scrambled eggs, home fries, and sausage gravy. The dessert menu features several tasty options, including sweet banana crepes.

The Mad Hatter has served up drinks and food to clients mad or not for thirty-four years. How do you survive over three decades in the restaurant business? "You serve hot food hot, cold food cold, and be nice," Tobin simply states. With a twenty-year lease at their new location, Tobin and Heisenberger plan to be in business for at least two more decades.

The Mad Hatter's website claims that people who wear hats tend to be a little different. From Charlie Chaplin to Pharrell Williams, they may be on to something. So grab a cap, fedora, or beret, and let your inner weirdo out at the Mad Hatter. You'll probably be in good, mad company.

MARTIN'S TAVERN

1264 WISCONSIN AVENUE NW • WASHINGTON, DC 20007

(202) 333-7370 • MARTINSTAVERN.COM

Bill (and Bill and Bill and Bill's) Excellent Adventure

We fought a war to free ourselves from monarchy, but Americans seem to long for their own royalty. It's why the E! network stays in business, why millions tuned in to watch William and Kate say "I do," and why the Kennedy family is so beloved.

Arguably the closest thing to royalty America has ever had, the Kennedy family has held offices from mayor to president and captivated Americans with their personal lives for decades. The most fascinating of duos in the Kennedy clan was JFK and Jackie. In 1951, Massachusetts senator John F. Kennedy and newspaper photographer Jackie Bouvier met at a dinner party in Georgetown. They dated for two years before getting engaged at Martin's Tavern.

A yellow building with black awnings on the corner of Wisconsin and N Street, Martin's Tavern has been a Georgetown staple since 1933.

John lived two blocks away and regularly popped in after church on Sundays to eat and read the newspaper. The "Rumble Seat," a nook for one, is named for his habit, and Madeleine Albright, Richard Nixon, and LBJ also have booths named for them.

But the Proposal Booth, where Jackie said yes on June 24, 1953, is the most romantic draw for customers and couples. In fact, Billy Martin, owner since 2001, estimates that twenty-five to thirty couples have gotten

engaged here in the last decade. Following in the footsteps of America's first "royal couple," whose wedding was compared to a coronation in *LIFE* magazine, is appealing to some modern couples.

The tavern is asymmetrical, with booths around the perimeter and crowded tables in the middle. The walls above the bar and in the back section called "the Dugout" are cluttered with photos of the tavern in years past, Martin family photos and crests, paintings of horses, and other random decorations, from a statue of a jockey to a plaque that reads, "All Our Visitors Bring Happiness. Some By Coming. Some By Going."

Billy's great-grandfather, William S. Martin, an Irish immigrant, and his son William G. opened the tavern in 1933. William G. was a Georgetown graduate and local celebrity who'd played professional basketball, football, and baseball. He even won a World Series with the Boston Braves in 1914. After his athletic career ended, he wanted to open a neighborhood tavern in his hometown but needed his father's help. As a resident of Arlington, Virginia, just across the Key Bridge from DC, William G. could not get a liquor license for a District business. But his father, a DC resident, could. So father and son teamed up and redecorated the Greek deli that once stood on the corner and opened a tavern on the heels of Prohibition's repeal.

"The reason it was so successful during the Depression was my family had very good connections with people up on the Hill," explains Billy. For instance, William G.'s close friend and Speaker of the House Sam Rayburn visited Martin's Tavern almost daily. "Back then," says Billy, Martin's was "the place to be." His father told him stories about four-star generals agreeing to sit on milk crates when the tavern was busy just so they wouldn't have to eat anywhere else.

In 1949, after serving in the navy and playing professional golf, William A. Martin joined the family business. He tended bar before taking ownership of Martin's.

Passing the business down to the next William was not a guarantee. "It was not something that I thought I would participate in," reflects Billy.

After his parents divorced when he was nine, Billy grew up in Florida, away from Martin's Tavern. But during a trip to DC at twenty-two, he unexpectedly decided to stay and bartend. "[I thought] oh, what the heck, why not," says Billy. "Once I got into it, I really liked it." Although he purchased the restaurant in 2001, Billy can still be found behind the bar from time to time, serving drinks and shucking clams.

The menu at Martin's Tavern consists of Martin family favorites, including family recipes for crab cakes, shepherd's pie, and meat loaf (Nixon's favorite). The menu offers plenty of comfort food and is extensive, including everything from oyster stew and seared ahi tuna to burgers and seafood lasagna.

Until two years ago, Martin's subsisted on line cooks. But Billy decided to bring in an executive chef to refine the menu to keep up with DC's burgeoning high-end restaurant industry. Improvements in quality and presentation create a perception of finer dining, but the prices remain affordable and true to Martin's commitment to serving the community.

The large menu offers enough variety to drive in customers several times a week. In addition to JFK, other regulars over the years have included Secretary of State Madeleine Albright, ABC News reporter Brit Hume, MSNBC's Chris Matthews, baseball player Mickey Mantle, and musician Mel Torme. Every president from Harry S. Truman to George W. Bush has also eaten at Martin's. Barack Obama has yet to visit, but the White House has contacted the tavern about getting him in the door before his term expires.

Billy has two teenage children, a daughter named Lauren and a son named Evan—just kidding: his name is Billy. Whether one of them continues the Martin family tradition or not, this Georgetown establishment will surely continue to serve the community its beloved food and ambience.

"The main thing that people like about Martin's is that it hasn't really changed," Billy imparts. Indeed, the comfort food and charming atmosphere have remained consistent since 1933. While the tavern hasn't changed much, life for dozens of patrons has. Like it was for JFK and Jackie, a meal at Martin's might be the start of a new partnership.

THE MONOCLE

107 D STREET NE • WASHINGTON, DC 20002

(202) 546-4488 • THEMONOCLE.COM

Congressional Cuisine

*J*f you want to dine like a member of Congress, head to the Monocle. Steps from the Capitol building, this sunny yellow restaurant is a favorite among those serving in the legislative branch.

While working as an accountant for several DC restaurants, Constantine Valanos kept suggesting that his clients renovate a property near the Capitol building. Instead, he did it himself, partnering with his wife, Helen.

The Greek-American duo opened the Monocle in 1960. "When my parents opened this location, there was not a nice fine dining restaurant on the Hill," reflects their son John Valanos, the current co-owner. "There was a void in the market."

Constantine and his wife ran the business for almost three decades. John intended to work in commercial real estate, but after filling in for various Monocle staff over the years, he grew to appreciate the restaurant more and more. "Before you know it, my parents were like, 'We're moving to Florida. Here are the keys.'"

And so the same year Taylor Swift was born (1989, for those of you living under a rock), they turned the reins over to John and his wife, Vasiliki.

"We've taken on the roles that his dad and mom had," says Vasiliki. Like his father, John runs things downstairs as the maître d'hôtel, and like John's mother, Vasiliki does the books upstairs. But "I didn't marry my mother," John quickly interjects.

John and Vasiliki met at the Monocle on a setup arranged by their parents. Vasiliki worked for a bank at the time, but once she got involved with John, she knew that the Monocle would draw her in. "Being in a Greek family, you know you're always involved in each other's business," she says. "We've been working together for twenty-one years."

And they make a good team. Trading playful smiles and lots of laughs while they speak about their restaurant with pride, it's clear that their love for the Monocle has made it a well-run and beloved institution on the Hill.

You are likely to see men and women in pinstripes and pencil skirts talking politics across tables draped with white tablecloths. The carpeted floor and wallpaper give the Monocle an upscale feel, but tourists in jeans and walking shoes are also welcome.

Those rocking suits or "I ♥ DC" shirts can benefit alike from the wise sayings written on the high beams of the restaurant: "If you can't feel things you can't see or hear, you don't belong here"; "If you want a friend in Washington . . . get a dog"; and the most appropriate for the venue, "An empty stomach is not a good political advisor."

Along with "my personality," John attributes the Monocle's success to a tradition of great service and high-quality cuisine. For members of Congress, the Monocle feels like "coming home," adds Vasiliki. Almost everywhere else, politicians have to worry about being photographed or that anything they say could go viral, but at the Monocle, members of Congress "feel comfortable." They are treated warmly but not invasively. The manager, Nick, is always up to date on what's going on in Congress. "He'll say things like, 'Great bill,' or 'What were you thinking?'" to congressional customers, says Vasiliki, but then they are given their privacy.

On the Monocle's fifty-fifth anniversary, members of Congress took over the restaurant. Tip O'Neill served as the maître d'hôtel and John Kerry served drinks behind the bar. In rotating shifts, the restaurant's famous customers became its staff.

The Monocle's American menu relies heavily on meat and seafood. The dinner menu features steak, lamb, pork, and chicken, along with salmon, clams, shrimp, and their well-reviewed crab cakes. Vegetarians can complement the one pasta dish on the menu with plenty of vegetable sides. The lunch menu adds salads and sandwiches. It's simple, tasty food.

While most things about the Monocle have remained constant since 1960, the food has improved. "The emphasis was on drinking back then," explains John. But today, in an age of global travel and organic everything, customers appreciate food more and more. Vasiliki says customers care about "the food quality, the preparation, [and] being innovative." The menu has adapted to those demands. The Monocle purchases fresh seafood daily, and the chef's daily specials offer creative dishes that don't interfere with the staples customers have come to expect and look forward to.

One additional, unfortunate change is "silence," John reports. In years past, John observed Republicans and Democrats dining together. But now "they don't talk to each other."

In the Monocle's early decades, secretaries called the Monocle to summon their representatives to vote. The Monocle's PA system would then call the rep back to the Capitol building. In the age of cell phones, that PA system is obsolete but still utilized. If you dine at the Monocle and pick up on any patrons' frenzy, the loudspeaker may confirm your suspicions of a vote. Unlike the radio star, it's a tradition that technology has not killed.

On some nights—perhaps after an important vote—the Monocle practically becomes a fraternity, with congressmen and women bouncing from table to table. It makes things tricky for a waiter trying to deliver orders, but it also infuses the Monocle with an exciting energy.

Ironically, the Monocle's clientele could potentially cause its undoing. The government forcibly purchased the Monocle (and the entire block) to have the option to construct an office building there. "Let's hope [nobody] gets a bad oyster," jokes John.

In the future, John hopes that the Monocle will become "a meeting place for both sides of Congress [where] they can come and share a meal together and find some common ground." The Valanoses have a son and daughter who will likely continue the family business. Perhaps by then that vision will take shape.

Welcome Guest!

You're at home now

That you like best.

All is yours

At home each minute.

Make yourselves

And all that's in it.

MRS. K'S TOLL HOUSE

RESTAURANT & BARREL BAR

9201 COLESVILLE ROAD • SILVER SPRING, MD 20910

(301) 589-3500 • MRSKS.COM

A Tasty Toll

*I*f all tollhouses looked like this one, more people would be excited about the New Jersey Turnpike. Alas, the idea of converting a toll-booth into a restaurant has yet to summon demand. However, a late nineteenth-century tollhouse in Montgomery County has summoned many to what it's been converted into: the charming Mrs. K's Toll House Restaurant and Barrel Bar.

Situated on a luscious parcel of property one mile north of the Silver Spring Metro stop, the restaurant's building served as the last operating tollhouse in Montgomery County. Horse-drawn carriages stopped to pay a four-cent toll at the house, lived in by a farmer who collected tolls in between farm duties. Once the toll was paid, travelers continued onto the privately owned Washington-Ashton Turnpike, also known as today's Route 29.

After the tollhouse closed, the house fell into a few different hands before DC restaurant owners Blanche and Harvey Kreuzburg purchased it in 1929. The couple wanted to open a new restaurant outside the city. On April 1, 1930, they opened Mrs. K's Toll House Tavern in the former tollhouse.

Blanche, aka "Mrs. K," used the new business to display her impressive antiques collection. Those antiques still fill the restaurant's many rooms today.

On the first floor, the Ben Franklin Room displays old china and drawings that deliver some of Franklin's famous maxims. Sayings like "When the well is dry they know the worth of water" and "Keep thy shop and thy shop will keep thee" can be found throughout the room, along with a fireplace whose mantel displays a row of antique pitchers.

Hidden off the Ben Franklin Room waits the Heirloom Corner, sometimes referred to as the Glass Room. Here Blanche's collection of pieces by famous glassblower Nicholas Lutz rest inside protective casings. Lutz, a Pennsylvanian by way of France, is best known for introducing threaded and striped designs to glassware, as well as for making paperweights.

The spacious main dining rooms on the first floor showcase Mrs. K's collection of Old Blue Staffordshire plates on high shelves along the perimeter of the room. Made in England between 1780 and 1830, these plates boast intricate blue designs and borders that function as the artist's signature.

The Terrace Dining Room features a treelike sculpture whose trunk is planted in the middle of the room and whose branches intertwine with lights on the ceiling in a circle. The effect is truly beautiful and creates an elegant atmosphere for dining.

Downstairs, the newer Barrel Bar has a more casual feel. Floors of brick and stone, low ceilings, and circular chandeliers full of candles create an intimate, fun atmosphere. True to its name, a few barrels are in view. The lower level is also home to Mrs. K's Wine Cellar, an addition in the last decade. The bar offers an extensive wine list alongside a plethora of whiskeys and local and craft beers.

Outside, the garden features a ginkgo tree that sprouts fruit in the summer and a copper beech tree that has been alive for more than fifty years. A white gazebo offers a romantic escape for couples, and a white archway on a small patio is a popular spot for wedding ceremonies. Afterward, many couples choose to hold their receptions in the Terrace Dining Room.

The Sunday all-you-can-eat buffet brunch is the most popular meal at Mrs. K's. From 10:30 to 2:30, Mrs. K's seats anywhere between 250 and 400 guests for a feast that includes carving and omelet stations, waffles, oysters, pastries, and more.

The most popular dinner dishes are the crab cakes, braised short ribs, and the New Zealand lamb chops, according to Mrs. K's assistant general manager, Andrew Parkin.

"Our clientele is an eclectic bunch," says Parkin. "We strive to make Mrs. K's a destination for [people of] all age group[s] and economic backgrounds." Happy hour wrangles the younger crowds downstairs to the Barrel Bar and Wine Cellar for drink specials and small bites, while older crowds with deeper pockets tend to enjoy finer dining upstairs.

In 1996, the Kreuzburgs sold Mrs. K's to Konstantina Margas, who passed it down to her brother, Spiro Gioldasis. The Margas family made their own wine in Greece, and Gioldasis brought this interest in wine to Mrs. K's. Under his leadership the wine cellar was constructed and the wine list greatly expanded.

For more than eighty-five years, Mrs. K's has served the Silver Spring and greater DC metro population. "I think one of the secrets [to Mrs. K's success] is our dedication over the years to our guests, providing great food and excellent service," says Parkin. Indeed, despite being a very busy restaurant, the front-of-house and serving staff treats its customers with warmth and care. Like the storied antiques that fill the restaurant, some of that staff has been with Mrs. K's for decades. Front-of-house manager Jane Harriman has been with Mrs. K's for forty years, catering director Tisheeka Wallace has been with the company for twenty years, and head chef Maurisee Upshur has been with Mrs. K's for eighteen years.

A mile up Colesville Road from the Silver Spring Metro station, Mrs. K's is a wonderfully rustic escape from the city. It'll cost you more than four cents, but it's worth the trip.

Vietnam in VA

Few restaurant owners can claim they were prisoners of war. But Nguyen Van Thoi is one who can. The founder of Clarendon restaurant Nam Viet, this man's life could be a Hollywood movie, and I call dibs.

After the fall of Saigon in 1975, the Communist government sent Thoi to a reeducation camp. He escaped from the camp after two years by paying a ransom. He and his family arranged to escape from Vietnam with about forty others by boat. The escapees arrived at the dock ready to sail to Thailand, but the captain never showed. Five-foot-tall Thoi wasn't taking no for an answer. He captained the ship himself.

Thoi and his family lived in Thailand for two years before immigrating to the United States through Catholic Charities. "Their vision of the American Dream did not initially start as a restaurant," says Thoi's son Richard, Nam Viet's current general manager. "[It] started as a vision to get my older brothers out of Vietnam and into the United States to get away from the Vietnam War." But opening Nam Viet in 1987 enabled the family to truly live the American Dream.

Nam Viet's location in Clarendon was perfect for an area then known as "Little Saigon." Many people left the area to escape a loud, long Metro construction. This drove rents down and enabled Vietnamese immigrants with little means to move in. Clarendon became a mini version of Plymouth Rock.

In total, 587 Americans were held as POWs in Asia during the Vietnam War. A good chunk of those faces are on the walls at Nam Viet. Every year,

Nam Viet hosts a dinner for American POWs around the Vietnamese New Year, called Tet. "It's an event that we look forward to every year," says Richard. Ironically, "Tet" recalls the Tet Offensive, a military strike during the Vietnam War that devastated the West.

The dinners began when Orson Swindle, a POW whose F-8 plane was shot down over Vietnam in 1966, made a reservation for fifteen POWs at the restaurant, not knowing Thoi's backstory. Thoi told him he was also a POW, and the men bonded. From then on, dinners were held at Nam Viet every year.

Tet held a special meaning for these American POWs: it was the one holiday their prison guards let them celebrate. While the food they ate on Tet was far from gourmet, it outshone the "sewer greens" they usually stomached. "It's a great time in which we get to see great heroes get together and reminisce about their time as servicemen and how as a family restaurant we continue to pay that great homage to longtime friends of my family," says Richard.

Dozens of military portraits hang near the entrance, including that of John McCain, arguably our nation's best-known POW. He signed his portrait "To Thoi—With appreciation for a delightful evening and all your sacrifices for the freedom of the Vietnamese people." Other signed pictures refer to Thoi as a hero, warrior, and friend.

Besides the military connection, authentic Vietnamese cuisine drives customers into Nam Viet. Thoi's wife, Ngoc Anh Tran, designed the menu and trained all the chefs. "My mother had always had a prowess for cooking," says Richard. "Every dish on the menu has my mother's distinct attention to detail."

Vietnamese cuisine has a significant French influence. France seized portions of Vietnam in the 1860s and extended their control over the country throughout the latter half of the century. Vietnamese cuisine's VIP is *pho*, a noodle soup whose name comes from *pot-au-feu,* or the French term for "beef stew." The Vietnamese also created their own version of a baguette with rice flour called *bánh mì*. This thin, crunchy take on French bread typically includes meat pâté, coriander, and pickled carrots. *Bo 7 món,* a seven-course beef dish created by the French after their occupation made beef more readily available, is still eaten in Vietnam. Sea snails, a traditional French ingredient, can be found in *bún ốc* soup. Cooking with butter and wine is also attributed to French influence.

Rice and fish sauce are the two stars of Vietnamese cuisine. Thoi and Ngoc actually descend from four generations of rice farmers in Can Tho, a tropical city in the Mekong Delta colloquially called the "bread basket of Southeast Asia." In 2014, Vietnam exported $4 billion in rice, which accounted for 20 percent of the world's rice trade. Fish sauce, aka *nước chấm,* is Vietnam's version of ketchup and mustard. The dipping sauce accompanies many dishes and traditionally contains lime juice, garlic, chilies, and sugar.

Nam Viet's food blends influences from France and Can Tho. Nam Viet's chefs season their dishes with traditional Vietnamese spices, chief among them cilantro, mint, lemongrass, and ginger. The lemongrass chicken sits

Vintage Spot
WHITLOW'S ON WILSON

Pick a nice day to try Whitlow's, a tiki bar in Clarendon that's been open since 1946. The rooftop bar has a thatched roof, wooden masks, surfboards, and heaters for chilly nights. Inside, paper lanterns and seascape murals join pool tables and a "sand bar" to continue the relaxed vibe mandated by tiki bars.

2854 Wilson Boulevard, Arlington, VA 22201,
(703) 276-9693, whitlows.com

on a bed of ghost-white noodles; nuts and shallots provide plenty of color and texture. The seafood salad mixes shrimp, calamari, and scallops with red onions, peanuts, mint, carrots, pickled daikon, cabbage, celery, and bell peppers in Nam Viet's homemade fish sauce. This fish sauce also tops the Vietnamese crepes made with mung beans and crispy spring rolls, about eight thousand of which Nam Viet serves weekly.

The menu includes many soups. In addition to *pho ga,* Nam Viet serves a crabmeat and asparagus soup, a spicy sweet-and-sour salmon soup, a flat egg noodle soup, and many more.

It's wholly possible to enjoy the food at Nam Viet without knowing the history of its founding family. But knowing that the *pho* you're enjoying had to journey from a Vietnamese POW camp to a clandestine boat to Thailand to DC before ending up in your bowl makes it all the more satisfying. You are truly slurping the American Dream.

OCCIDENTAL GRILL & SEAFOOD

1475 PENNSYLVANIA AVENUE NW • WASHINGTON, DC 20004

(202) 783-1475 • OCCIDENTALDC.COM

Hungry for Peace

*C*rab cakes and a pork chop with a side of crisis management. Not your typical order, but on one historic day at the Occidental Grill & Seafood, it's exactly what was on the menu.

It was October of 1962. The Cold War had pitted the United States and the USSR against one another. It was Kennedy versus Khrushchev in the battle for Communist containment or expansion. Fidel Castro had seized power in Cuba and allied himself with the Soviet Union, and a month earlier, the USSR had shipped nuclear missiles to Cuba. Less than two hundred miles off the coast of Florida, Cuba's new missiles were in position to strike the United States.

The United States set up a blockade around Cuba. No ships could get in or out. But their missiles could still hit us, and our secret missiles in Turkey and Italy could still reach them. Two superpowers were on the brink of nuclear war in the Cuban Missile Crisis.

Cut to the Occidental Grill & Seafood. Two blocks from the White House, ABC News journalist John A. Scali accepted Aleksandr "Mr. X" Fomin's lunch invitation, even though he'd already eaten. Scali ordered crab cakes. Mr. X ordered the pork chop and offered a deal: if the Soviets removed the missiles from Cuba, would the United States promise never to invade Cuba without direct provocation? Fomin asked Scali to pass this offer along to President Kennedy. To protect their objectivity, journalists are not supposed to get involved in the stories they're covering. Luckily, Scali put homeland

security above professional ethics. For the next few days, Scali acted as a go-between to officially broker this deal between the United States and the USSR that resolved the crisis.

A plaque above the booth where Scali and Fomin ate commemorates the important lunch. Even though the food was secondary—Scali ate Mr. X's pork chop and Mr. X ate Scali's crab cakes without realizing the mix-up—it was a lunch for the ages.

The Occidental's history began six decades before its pivotal role in the Cold War. Henry Willard, of the adjacent Willard Hotel, built the Occidental in 1906. Six years later, Gustav Bucholz purchased the restaurant. When World War I broke out, Bucholz, a German immigrant, displayed his American allegiance by donated the proceeds from the coatroom to the Red Cross, and by encouraging customers to respect the rationing in effect. He added a note in the menu: *"Mr. Hoover says: 'To win the war we must conserve our food.' During these war times we ask the cooperation of our patrons in the avoidance of all waste in the food supply."*

After Gustav died at fifty, he passed the restaurant down to his son Frederick, who ran operations for two decades. The restaurant fell on hard times in the late 1960s and had to close in 1971. It did not reopen until 1986 in a new location steps from the original, sporting the same decor.

Portraits of the five most recent presidents greet you at the entrance. If you look closely at President George W. Bush, you may notice that his hands seem a bit large and his shoulders a bit wide. That's because the painter began painting before the election, assuming that Al Gore would win. Rather than start over, he simply added Bush's head to the body he'd started. And if you think that the ring painted on Bill Clinton's finger looks fresher than the rest of the paint, there's a reason: the artist originally painted Bill without his wedding ring. But after the Lewinsky scandal broke, he returned to the Occidental and added the ring. Even painters have to do damage control in DC.

The restaurant's first floor is split-level. Six spacious, comfortable booths occupy the first level. A few steps below on the main level, round tables and booths are backdropped by delightfully cluttered walls of famous faces. Huge portraits of Helen Keller, Martin Luther King Jr., Amelia Earhart, Will Rogers, JFK, Margaret Chase Smith, Eleanor Roosevelt, and Jackie Robinson are spaced out along the perimeter of the restaurant. In between them, dozens of other portraits are arranged like neatly laid bricks, leaving little blank space anywhere. Swing and jazz classics play in the background, and the bar TV broadcasts CNN. The hardwood floors and wood paneling create a sense of refinement and power, along with the white tablecloths and miniature lamps at each booth.

Upstairs in the wine room, horizontally stacked bottles of Merlot and Chardonnay create a darker, more intimate feel than the rows of portraits eyeing you in the main area. Also upstairs, plush carpets and presidential portraits create a classy setting for meetings in the Monument and Presidential Rooms. Outside, the courtyard offers a more relaxed vibe under striking blue umbrellas. Overall, the dignified decor of the Occidental warrants its motto: "Where Statesmen Dine."

The food is decidedly upscale but not outlandishly priced. You can expect to pay around $30 for a dinner entree. Executive chef Rodney Scruggs, whose history with the Occidental began as an eighteen-year-old line cook, has created a stunning menu. The duck is marinated in honey vinegar; served with savoy cabbage, carrots, and burnt golden raisins; and topped with a foie gras sauce. The grilled yellowfin tuna is served with sweet potato, black quinoa, an herb puree, and a pomegranate reduction. The lunch menu includes sandwiches and salads. I enjoyed the grilled chicken sandwich on fluffy focaccia bread with a hearty wedge of brie, and vegetarians will enjoy the ricotta pesto cavatelli or the sautéed spaghetti squash.

The stakes of your meal might not be as high as John A. Scali's, but without the weight of the world on your shoulders, you're sure to enjoy your time at the Occidental.

OFF THE RECORD

AT THE HAY-ADAMS
800 16TH STREET NW • WASHINGTON, DC 20006
(202) 638-2716 • HAYADAMS.COM

Cartoon Cuisine

I put my glass of soda down on a coaster featuring a cartoon of Michelle Obama giving Chris Christie the stink eye as he's about to devour a juicy hamburger and plate of fries. I doubt the First Lady of Health would condone my Diet Coke, so it's a good thing she's 2-D.

The cartoon is an original from Pulitzer Prize–winning political cartoonist Matthew Wuerker of *Politico*, whose work is featured throughout Off the Record alongside cartoons by *The Economist*'s Kevin Kallaugher, Richard Thompson, and the *Washington Post* Pulitzer Prize winner Ann Telnaes.

Located in the basement of the Hay-Adams hotel steps from the White House, Off the Record is an upscale power bar that celebrates the best and worst of Washington politics in caricature. During the day, the bar is relatively quiet. But after 5 p.m., congressmen, staffers, bankers, and other Washington movers and shakers take over the velvety red booths and octagonal bar.

Off the Record is somewhat "off the record." As a basement bar, you won't stumble on it while exploring the neighborhood. With bartenders who've been here for decades and know them, prominent political figures feel comfortable at Off the Record.

The menu is short and sweet. In particular, patrons enjoy the generously sized martinis and Manhattans. The menu features appetizers such as the

popular pork buns and crystal shrimp dumplings, salads, sandwiches, and entrees like grilled chicken with creamy polenta and grilled rockfish fillet.

But the real draw is the decor. Two walls of older black-and-white caricatures grace the back corner, while newer, rotating pieces decorate the other walls.

Some gems include Kevin Kallaugher's caricature of Donald Trump placing a replica of his blonde toupee on an elephant wearing a "2012" sticker. Other cartoons by Kallaugher, aka KAL, include Barack Obama getting advice from a portrait of Ronald Reagan and Mitt Romney looking in a mirror but seeing the reflection of his running mate, Paul Ryan. Ann Telnaes's long, angular caricatures depict a very defeated-looking Mitt Romney at a podium and a sketch of a very triumphant-looking Barack and Michelle Obama holding hands and waving to supporters. Matt Wuerker's cartoons include a shirtless Dick Cheney in boxing gloves ready to fight.

"I got a call from the Hay-Adams," recalls Wuerker. The bar was well known for its black-and-white caricatures from collector Art Wood, but the subjects were out of date. "It was becoming a problem, because the clientele wasn't recognizing the caricatures anymore," Wuerker explains. So Off the Record displayed more current work by Richard Thompson. "Richard said, 'Call up my friend Matt,'" says Wuerker.

So Wuerker met with the Hay-Adams and struck a deal: cartoons for bourbon. Once or twice a month, Wuerker cashes in on his booze contract and enjoys a Knob Creek bourbon at Off the Record.

Every six months, Wuerker and KAL draw about six new cartoons featuring headline-making politicians inside Off the Record. "The idea is to capture who's in the news and put them in the bar," Wuerker explains. Wuerker's coasters feature Rand Paul drinking from a "T Party" tea bag and gazing longingly at a picture of the White House, four generations of the Bush family gathered gingerly in an Off the Record booth, and a sketch of Bill Clinton serving as Hillary's roadie as she charges out of the Hay-Adams.

KAL's coasters include Barack Obama enjoying a glass of wine, poured from behind the bar by none other than George W. Bush.

Cartoons that poke fun at politicians are even enjoyed by the politicians at the butt of the joke. "Most politicians that I've met, they get the joke, know it comes with the territory," says Wuerker. "I'll get requests from people that are the subjects asking for copies," he elaborates. He lists "greedy, stupid politicians" and "the power of money in politics" as two subjects he most enjoys drawing. But don't expect to see any blatantly offensive cartoons on Off the Record's walls. The work on the walls is critical without being offensive, funny without being crude.

In the shadow of the *Charlie Hebdo* massacre, Wuerker argues, "I don't think going and drawing Muhammad as a dog makes you a champion of free speech." Just like cartoonists who draw "yucky" cartoons for *Hustler*, Wuerker believes in a cartoonist's right to draw anything he or she wants, and his right to dislike it.

And as for cartoons' appeal, Wuerker thinks it's here to stay. "We live in an [age of] incredibly short attention spans," he says. Indeed, digesting a political cartoon is like speed-reading a newspaper article with an added bonus of humor.

As the 2016 election approaches, be prepared for new cartoons at Off the Record featuring a new president. For cartoonists, a new president is bittersweet. "There's a certain kind of dread [that] you're going to have to learn someone's face," Wuerker says. Whoever wins the Oval Office in 2016, you're sure to see their exaggerated features on the walls of Off the Record.

Off the Record is a classy spot to order a big drink and eavesdrop on its exciting mix of patrons. Matt Wuerker put it best: "[DC] is a fascinating town to get to work in, and working at *Politico* gives me a front-row seat; hanging out at the Hay-Adams gives me a front-row bar stool."

OLD ANGLER'S INN

10801 MACARTHUR BOULEVARD • POTOMAC, MD 20854

(301) 365-2425 • OLDANGLERSINN.COM

Canal Cooking

The Old Angler's Inn has served Washingtonians since 1860. But it's most famous for who it *hasn't* served.

In 1961, proprietor Olympia Reges kicked out Supreme Court Justice William Douglas, along with his entourage of congressmen and press. She'd just put a new carpet inside the restaurant. Chief Douglas and his associates, all dripping wet from an excursion on the canal across the street, brought their own lunches into the restaurant and ordered only water. "She comes flying down the spiral staircase to see these three men . . . dripping on her new carpet," laughs her son Mark, the current co-owner. She ordered the dirty, nonspending group to get out. "The next day, my father was trying a case in Miami, Florida, and the front-page headline is 'Innkeeper's Wife Kicks Out Justice Douglas.'"

Olympia had no idea whom she'd thrown out, but soon the entire country did. National papers picked up the story, and news of this fiery woman spread from coast to coast. At first, Olympia worried the story would have a negative effect on business. Chief Justice Earl Warren contacted Olympia and assured her that she had been well within her rights. He gave Olympia his phone number and told her to call if anyone gave her any trouble. But she never needed to call. The business losses she anticipated turned instead into gains: "People started lining up to see who this woman was," says Mark.

Today I hope the headline would have described Olympia as the "innkeeper," not the "innkeeper's *wife*." Sexism aside, business boomed.

Olympia's feisty persona drew crowds in, and she capitalized on it. "Coke went up from five cents to a dollar fifty," says Mark.

The Old Angler's Inn dates back to 1860. During the Civil War, travelers and soldiers from both the North and South stopped here. In 1957, John and Olympia Reges enjoyed lunch at Angler's. Olympia loved it so much that John bought it. Busy with his work as a lawyer, John told Olympia, "You've got to do it on your own," recalls Mark. And she did. Through the 1980s, Olympia ruled Angler's with an iron fist. "She was the spark of Angler's," says Mark.

Angler's became especially popular for clandestine, romantic meetings between bosses and secretaries. "You would have thirty reservations and sixty cars in the parking lot," recalls Mark. "The boss would be in one car and the secretary in the other. What happened at Angler's stayed at Angler's."

But as Bethesda grew and DC's restaurant scene roared, the Old Angler's Inn faded from people's minds. The restaurant struggled in the last years of Olympia's life. After she passed away in 2005, her sons stepped in to revitalize the restaurant.

Today the restaurant features several sections with distinct environments. Outside in the front, swing music plays from a rock that sneakily doubles as a speaker on the two-tiered patio. In the back, the beer garden offers a more casual option and live music. Unlike his mother, Mark welcomes people in sweaty clothes from the canal, and the beer garden is the perfect place to put them.

Older people should stay outside and on the first floor of the restaurant, because the spiral staircase to access the second floor is difficult to maneuver. Mark acknowledges the staircase's role in their demographic shift. "Most of the original clientele are either dead or not ambulatory enough to get up the spiral staircase," he reckons. Whereas the average age of clients was once sixty-five, Angler's now targets patrons from thirty-five to sixty, generally speaking. But eighty-five is the new sixty-five, so fear not, senior citizens: on a nice day, there is plenty of room on the spacious patio and first floor.

On the cozy first floor, black-and-white-checkered tablecloths cover six tables. A smooth, black marble bar seats about ten, and a crackling fire creates a charming atmosphere designed by Mark's wife Sarah, a co-owner.

Upstairs, murals of fishing scenes grace the walls. These murals were once hidden under plaster. But after a leak, the plaster began to fade, revealing the paintings. Mark's grandfather painted some of these scenes, and others date back to 1910.

The menu is on the pricier side with American dinner entrees from $19 to $38. The New York strip is twenty-one days aged in a red wine sauce and comes with wild mushrooms, potatoes, and a carrot puree. The menu features several fish items, such as an organic salmon in a sweet-and-sour mustard sauce, a Chesapeake Bay rockfish, and caramelized scallops served with sweet potato hash, bacon, brussels sprouts, and roasted chestnuts. Meat dishes include the chef's signature meatballs, a chicken dish with roasted acorn squash, and a shepherd's pie. The lunch menu adds sandwiches, the brunch menu features classic breakfast items, and the dessert menu boasts innovative items like a pumpkin crème brûlée and a rosemary and fig cake. The bar also has a selection of single-malt Scotches, brandies, bourbons, and sherries.

By 2017, Mark expects the final stage in rebranding to be complete: an inn. "We turn away so many requests for private events because we don't have the facility," he says. But with the addition of an inn and banquet hall up the hill from the patio, those requests can be met.

For the last ten years, revitalizing Angler's has been a challenge for Mark and his family. "As an attorney, in hindsight, quite frankly, I probably would have been better advising the estate to sell [Angler's]," he admits. But now that he and Sarah are on the other side of all the hard work, he's glad he stuck with it.

"I kept this place, really more than any other reason, because I grew up here," says Mark. "My family's history is here."

Hike the canal and then be a part of that history. Just wipe your feet first.

OLD EBBITT GRILL

675 15TH STREET NW • WASHINGTON, DC 20005

(202) 347-4800 • EBBITT.COM

The Oldest Saloon in the City

As you push through a revolving door to enter the Old Ebbitt Grill, you will probably be met with a full house. Two thousand guests dine at this restaurant on a daily basis and have been doing so since 1856.

The Old Ebbitt originated as a boardinghouse run by William E. Ebbitt in 1856. Many important movers and shakers called it home. While in Congress, for example, future president William McKinley lived at the house. Ulysses S. Grant, Andrew Johnson, Grover Cleveland, Teddy Roosevelt, and Warren Harding are just a few of the esteemed men who socialized at the boardinghouse's bar.

A walrus head hunted by Theodore Roosevelt hangs in the Old Ebbitt Grill. President Roosevelt loved hunting for sport and for scientific research. After his second presidential term ended in 1909, the Smithsonian commissioned Roosevelt to safari through Africa for eleven months. During that time, he trapped and shot more than eleven thousand animals, including elephants, hippos, and rhinos. This haul started the Smithsonian's Natural History Museum.

Wooden bears purchased by Alexander Hamilton also reside at the Old Ebbitt Grill, along with bird prints by well-known painter Robin Hill.

The Ebbitt is divided into many unique rooms, creating a flow that keeps crowded nights feeling energized instead of overwhelming. The main dining room hosts the greatest number of guests, and additional seating is

available in the Atrium dining room and downstairs in the Cabinet Room, both of which are great for weddings or private events. The Old Ebbitt Grill also has four bars: the Old Bar, Oyster Bar, Corner Bar, and Grant's Bar. It takes one hundred kitchen employees to keep this Death Star fully operational.

In 1970, ownership switched hands to Stuart Davidson and John Laytham, the owners of Clyde's in Georgetown (also profiled in this book). After falling on hard times, the Old Ebbitt Grill hosted an auction to benefit their struggling business. Davidson and Laytham attended. When the auction's proceeds fell short of what the Old Ebbitt needed to stay afloat, the owners surprised everyone by putting the restaurant itself up for sale. Clyde's restaurateurs walked away with a new property for $11,200, the first addition to their restaurant empire in the Washington area.

The Ebbitt has been popular for well over a century. When word leaked that William McKinley was to stay at the Ebbitt House before his inauguration, the masses descended on the Old Ebbitt hoping for a reservation. Buffalo Bill, who parlayed his experiences riding for the Pony Express into the "Buffalo Bill's Wild West" cowboy show that toured the country, visited the Ebbitt in 1891. The eatery shifted locations a few times before moving to its current spot near the White House in 1983. Secret Service members have been known to hang out at the Ebbitt, and protestors marching on the nearby Washington Mall often end up at the Ebbitt after exercising their freedom of speech.

The menu is upscale and priced reasonably well. The average dinner entree will set you back around $18. The lunch and dinner menus are comparable and varied. Duck, salmon, steak, and cannelloni entrees are fancier than a separate sandwich menu that includes burgers, sandwiches, and catfish tacos. A large cheese sampler is available to start, and beautiful salads are filled with ingredients like kale, cranberries, quinoa, frisée, farro, and radicchio and topped with unique dressings like apple cider and sherry vinaigrettes.

The Old Ebbitt Grill is a popular choice for brunch. The menu makes french toast special by infusing it with apples and honey pecan butter. The pork schnitzel douses a fried pork cutlet in a bacon-mushroom gravy with spätzle (egg noodles) and sunny-side-up eggs. Of course, the menu includes standard brunch items like fried chicken and waffles, crab cakes, and quiche.

The Old Ebbitt's four bars also serve plenty of wines, whiskeys, beers, and cocktails to those partaking in the establishment's busy nightlife. An extensive late-night menu accommodates post-dinner munchies.

An entirely separate oyster menu features seven variations along the briny-sweet spectrum: $29.95 gets you a dozen, and $16.95 gets you a half dozen. If you have serious dough to spend or haven't eaten in several days, try the Orca Platter. This $126.95 two-tiered dish includes twenty-four oysters, twelve shrimp, six clams, six crab claws, and one lobster perched at the top.

Every year, the Ebbitt hosts the International Wines for Oysters Competition. Winemakers from across the globe submit their wines. Prominent judges have included Supreme Court Justice Antonin Scalia. The best ten wines go on to be featured at the Ebbitt's annual Oyster Riot. During this two-day festival the Friday and Saturday before Thanksgiving, about ten thousand attendees polish off more than seventy thousand oysters. The Ebbitt offers the winning wine at the restaurant for the next year.

The Old Ebbitt operates in a building that once housed B. F. Keith's Theatre. Today inside the Beaux Arts building, you'll see a different sort of performance: the hard work from servers and bartenders it takes to pull off an establishment of this size, the awkward dances of couples on first dates, the hushed conversation of people talking about their classified jobs, and much more. The Old Ebbitt's walls tell the story of its historic beginnings, its political guests, and its status as the oldest bar in the city. So squeeze in and be a part of history.

OLD EUROPE

2434 WISCONSIN AVENUE NW • WASHINGTON DC 20007

(202) 333-7600 • OLD-EUROPE.COM

A Taste of Germany

*A*t Old Europe, *Gemütlichkeit* comes with everything on the menu. Meaning "friendliness" in German, *Gemütlichkeit* embodies the attitude of this Georgetown restaurant. Schnitzel and sausage dishes have come with a side of friendliness at Old Europe since 1948.

When Hitler rose to power in 1933, the Lichtenstein family saw the writing on the wall and fled Germany. The Jewish family relocated in Uruguay and Chicago before settling in Washington, DC. In the late 1940s, the Concord Club, a social group for Washingtonians of German descent, longed for a restaurant to serve as their home base. "Papa Lichtenstein," as he was known, partnered with the Concord Club and opened Old Europe in 1948.

For two decades, Papa Lichtenstein ran the restaurant with his sons Auto and Hans. As Jews who felt lucky to have escaped concentration camps, the Lichtensteins valued fair and equal treatment of all. "They did not tolerate any kind of segregation," says Old Europe's current owner, Alex Herold. Customers of any faith or race were welcomed, and anyone who had a problem with Old Europe's open-door policy was asked to leave.

The Lichtenstein family ran Old Europe until 1970, when Karl Herold took over, succeeded by his son Alex. Alex's family has always had a close relationship with the Lichtensteins. His parents met through family acquaintances of the Lichtensteins. "Somebody played Cupid there," says Alex. Alex is a first-generation Washingtonian. Karl left Germany before the Berlin Wall divided his family between East and West German. Alex's father and

mother, a Spaniard, imbued in him a love of German culture. As a child, he spent many summers in Europe. As an adult, Alex underwent eight years of culinary training before returning to DC to run Old Europe.

The restaurant's decor is striking and thematic. Waitresses dress in traditional German clothing. Oil paintings the Lichtensteins brought with them from Germany cover the walls, depicting landscapes and portraits of men and women enjoying libations. Interspersed between these paintings stand antique beer steins that depict phrases, limericks, and scenes of drinking and merriment. Most are one of a kind. The family also brought a beautiful cuckoo clock with them from Germany. More than 125 years old, it hangs in a corner and has been restored to bring out colors once dulled by smoke damage. Crisscrossed guns and antlers poke out of the top. Model ships that the Lichtensteins acquired at various DC flea markets also hang from the restaurant's ceiling. A nod to Germany's rich shipbuilding tradition, these boats look like miniature versions of the *Black Pearl*.

Be sure to look up to where coats of arms and seals of German states and principalities grace the ceiling. The Lichtensteins commissioned an artist to paint these squares in the late 1950s. Crests of European countries also join the landscapes and portraits, spreading the love not only for Germany but for other European countries such as Portugal, France, and Spain.

The menu features classic German cuisine prepared by Alex's wife, Cindy Herold, a German chef. "The schnitzel dishes [and] the sausage dishes are always the most popular," reports Alex. The sausage platter features three types of sausage: veal, pork, and smoked beef and pork. The platter comes with delicious mashed potato balls dripping in a savory gravy that contains a hint of sweet Marsala, along with onions and sauerkraut. Three mustards accompany the sausage, two imported from Germany and one house-made. The veal sausage goes especially well with the sweet mustard. The house recipe has "been around forever," according to Alex, and its mustard seeds add a nice texture to any of the bratwursts.

Old Europe offers special seasonal items. In the spring, Old Europe features pounds of green and white asparagus as a side dish. "In Europe, asparagus are considered the king of vegetables," explains Alex. During DC's Cherry Blossom Festival, the menu incorporates cherries. In the winter months, venison, duck, and "all the little furry things" are particularly popular, according to Alex. Year-round, the wine and beer list features seventy-five German wines and classic German beers served in generous clear mugs or boots.

Of course, Oktoberfest draws especially big crowds. Old Europe serves around twelve thousand people from mid-September to mid-November and caters many Oktoberfest celebrations. During the famous festival, Old Europe's three floors are full of beer and schnitzel enthusiasts. The rest of the year, German clubs often use the restaurant's second floor or lower level for meetings.

The restaurant serves many customers with ties to Germany, like army veterans who spent time in Germany during the war and people from the German, Austrian, and Swiss embassies. Famous visitors have included Robert De Niro and Donald Rumsfeld. Locals and students from nearby Georgetown, George Washington, and American Universities also frequent the restaurant, often with parents visiting from out of town. Tour groups and schools also sometimes wind up at Old Europe after visiting the Holocaust Museum. The restaurant gets its fair share of German tourists who are "tired of pizza and want to feel at home" too, says Alex.

The German ambience achieved with decor and food is completed with German music. For the last five years, an Austrian duo plays live polka music every Wednesday night. On Saturdays and Mondays, live piano music joins the sound waves of jovial chatter throughout the restaurant.

Whether it's a party of one or sixty, Alex wants "to make everyone feel like they're the king [or] the queen. They're here to be pampered [and] have a good time." If spicy schnitzel and German beer is your idea of a good time, set sail for Old Europe.

THE PALM

1225 19TH STREET NW • WASHINGTON, DC 20036
202) 293-9091 • THEPALM.COM

Will Draw for Food

I t's a common threat that if you don't pay for your food at a restaurant, you'll be put to work washing dishes. But there are other options. With a little negotiation, you could draw your way out of a bill. That's what a group of cartoonists did at the Palm, a refined white-tablecloth restaurant with locations across the United States. The first Palm opened in New York in 1926, and the second of twenty-eight locations opened in Washington, DC, in 1972.

Pio Bozzi and John Ganzi immigrated to the United States from Parma, Italy, in 1920. They decided to open a steak house together and wanted to call it "Parma." But their Italian accents made it sound like "Palm," and the Palm was born on Second Avenue. Jackets and ties were required of men in the upscale restaurant.

In the 1940s, the duo's sons took over. Walter Ganzi and Bruno Bozzi popularized the "surf and turf" cuisine by adding a two-pound lobster to the menu. During World War II, high-quality red meat became scarce, as most of it was sent to U.S. Army bases for our soldiers. The illegal meat trade surged during a time when most Americans had to settle for subpar beef, pork, and poultry. But for patriotic Americans who didn't want to get their meat on the black market, the Palm was a saving grace. The restaurant enjoyed a period of particular popularity at this time, as it was able to acquire and sell the high-quality meat Americans so desperately craved.

In 1963, Walter and Bruno dropped the suit and tie requirement at the Palm, paving the way for a more casual but still upscale dining experience. Two years later, the Palm added a four-pound lobster to the menu. The years of "bigger is better" had begun, and lobsters sold like hotcakes.

The Palm decided to expand at the suggestion of George H. W. Bush in the 1970s. Bush Sr. had dined at the Palm in New York and encouraged Walter and Bruno to open a Palm in the capital. They went forward with the plan and enlisted Tommy Jacomo's help.

A thirty-three-year veteran of DC's Palm, Jacomo left his job at a Vermont ski lodge to build the Washington, DC, Palm with his brother in 1972. The job was to last a few weeks. "Thirty three years later I'm still here," he says. Jacomo had followed in his father's footsteps and worked as a barback and bartender in New York City. He slipped back into that role at the Palm before becoming the manager and current executive director. He's currently at work on a book about his experiences at the Palm called *Nobody Knows the Truffles I've Seen*.

One of those notable "truffles" involves sparring with Muhammad Ali inside the restaurant. "He initiated the whole thing," recalls Jacomo. Jacomo's friend represented Ali at the time and brought him to the Palm. After they met, Ali started boxing with Jacomo, an avid boxing fan. Who won? "Oh, he won," confirms Jacomo.

Pictures of Jacomo and Ali hang on the walls at the Palm, but the walls *themselves* are a sight to behold. Cartoons cover practically every inch of space. Cartoonists who couldn't pay their bill started the tradition of covering the walls in caricatures in New York, but the tradition lives on. (However, I wouldn't recommend bringing your markers in lieu of your wallet today.)

Some eleven thousand to twelve thousand caricatures cover the DC Palm walls, Jacomo estimates. Most are prominent lawyers and lobbyists. Jacomo's favorite is author Norman Mailer. When space ran out on the walls, they started drawing on the ceiling. And few if any have ever been removed.

Jacomo wants to avoid grandchildren coming in to see their grandfather's picture only to ask, "Where's Poppy?"

Over the years, the clientele's preferences have changed. "There's no more three-martini lunch," says Jacomo. Instead patrons generally like to sip on white wine and sparkling water. Thanks to the popularity of cooking shows and food culture, customers have also become much more in tune with what they're eating. "I have fifteen thousand Gordon Ramsays," jokes Jacomo of his clientele. Health-conscious diners have also become more prevalent. "I never even heard of gluten-free twenty years ago," he says. Now it's hard to miss. "We accommodate whatever the guests want," he says.

For the most part, that's meat. The Palm's best known for its filet mignon, rib-eye, and New York strip. Add a lobster to anything from the steak and chops section of the menu for half price to get your surf and turf on. The menu also includes several classic Italian dishes, paying homage to the restaurant's Italian roots. But here, meat rules, so there's no spaghetti and meatballs or lasagna. Instead, veal marsala, chicken parmigiana, and veal Milanese represent the European boot.

Other than meat and "my charming personality," Jacomo says the Palm's "consistency of the product" drives customers inside. So does the service. "I love the interaction with the people," Jacomo says. "They become family over the years."

While American diners have embraced cuisine from all over the world in the last forty years, meat and potatoes have not yet gone out of style. And if you're on the Ron Swanson diet, paddle your handmade canoe to the Palm.

PARKWAY DELI

8317 GRUBB ROAD • SILVER SPRING, MD 20910

(301) 587-1427 • THEPARKWAYDELI.COM

"I'm going to marry a Jewish woman because I like the idea of getting up Sunday morning and going to the deli." —Michael J. Fox

*P*arkway Deli sits in a strip mall on an appropriately named street: Grubb Road. True to name, grub abounds inside the Jewish deli's doors. But its name really comes from the deli's proximity to Rock Creek Park. Three miles from the Silver Spring subway station, Parkway Deli's the kind of neighborhood joint where Girl Scouts sell cookies and people of all ages gather to dine and catch up.

Lou Gurewitz opened Parkway Deli in 1963 with his sister Rose and her husband, Mike. The space had previously been a popular hangout for teens on weekend nights, complete with a jukebox and dance floor. Lou's son Stuart took over in Parkway 1974, and today his sons Danny and Gary run the business.

Lou and his sons grew up in Brooklyn, New York. New York's most famous deli, Katz's Deli—home of "I'll have what she's having"—has a presence in the Gurewitz family's deli. Several unique framed collages use raised materials to create scenes of New York, including Katz's.

Danny, Parkway's current president, did not have an obvious route to the family business. He moved to Houston as a boy when his parents

divorced, so he didn't spend much time at the deli. When his mother passed away, he moved back to the DC area and started working for Lou in 1991. Danny had previously studied nuclear engineering in college, but on a good day, he doesn't have to put that knowledge to use at Parkway. In 2005, he took over as president when Lou had a stroke.

The atmosphere at Parkway Deli is like a mullet: business up front, party in the back. The entrance leads into a deli counter and a few rows of groceries. Continue walking back to get to the seating area. Freshly painted purple, green, and blue walls give it a vibrant feel, and large, black booths provide comfortable seating.

Danny views Parkway as a "homey home away from home." Judging by its clientele on a busy Saturday afternoon, many people feel that way about the deli. The weekend crowd includes old and young, black, white, and Asian customers, and families and couples. According to Danny, the clientele is an "incredible mix" from "all walks of life." Many customers who grew up coming to Parkway now bring in their kids.

The restaurant's food feels more upscale than the word "deli" conveys. It's full of paninis, wraps, subs, and burgers. The delicious Monterey Chicken Panini blends ham, chicken, cheese, and a hint of ranch on a slightly crunchy toasted roll. Dinner fare includes chicken, turkey, and seafood dishes.

And what would a deli be without breakfast? Bagels abound, many accompanied by fish, from kippered salmon to smoked Alaskan black cod on bagels with cream cheese, lettuce, tomato, and other goodies.

The Gurewitz family has peppered the menu with various Jewish dishes as well. The deli sells about three hundred pounds of corned beef a week, and pastrami, brisket, chopped liver, and tongue can be bought as well. The deli also sells plenty of potato pancakes, knish, cold borscht, baked stuffed cabbage, kosher dogs, and cheese blintzes topped with applesauce or sour cream. The matzo ball soup is also one of the restaurant's best-selling and best-reviewed dishes.

Dessert menus at each booth highlight two dozen cakes, pies, cheese-cakes, ice cream, and pastries.

Meals come with access to a pickle bar. "Delis and pickles go hand in hand," reasons Danny. As a kid, Danny bused tables, and he used to give each party a bowl of pickles and sauerkraut. "I guess over the years my dad got the idea and added all these things to the pickle bar, and people loved it." The complimentary pickle bar features crisp pickled beets, peppers, cauliflower, and tomatoes in addition to pickled cucumbers.

The Parkway Deli has thrived in a bad time for Jewish delis. Since their height of popularity between 1920 and the 1970s, Jewish delis have largely been closing. In the late 1800s, Jewish immigrants who were trying to assimilate to American culture shied away from embracing traditional Jewish foods. But in the early twentieth century, as Jews started being seen as Americans instead of immigrants, they embraced Jewish cuisine and delis boomed. However, after a few decades of prominence, Jewish delis began to close one after another. One culprit is an increasingly health-conscious culture that discourages consumption of goose- and chicken-fat-fried foods common in Jewish cuisine. Faster, cheaper options also shoulder blame. High-quality deli meats may outrank fast-food subs from Quiznos or Subway, but fast-food subs satisfy busy workers on their lunch breaks quicker and for less money. Delis have also become less popular within Jewish communities, especially with younger Jews who have embraced many new cuisines along with Americans in general.

While other delis have closed their doors, Danny expects the business to stay in the family for years to come. "I have three boys," he says of his children, ages nine, three, and a newborn. "Most likely one of them is going to want to keep it going." If our current child labor laws remain intact, that will be a few million pounds of corned beef from now. Judging by a busy Saturday afternoon crowd, Parkway will certainly get there.

PEKING GOURMET INN

CULMORE SHOPPING CENTER, 6029 LEESBURG PIKE

FALLS CHURCH, VA 22041

(703) 671-8088 • PEKINGGOURMET.COM

Ducks for Dinner

A server brings a duck to the table. With careful knife strokes, he separates pieces of tender meat and crispy skin. He places these pieces of duck on a thin pancake along with cucumber and onion sticks and then drizzles hoisin sauce on top before rolling it into a texture-filled wrap. The duck inside this crepe is one of seventy thousand that the Peking Gourmet Inn sells each year and is but one of many delectable Chinese dishes available at this Falls Church gem.

Eddie Tsui opened the Peking Gourmet Inn in 1978. Wooden partitions are artfully mounted on the walls, traditional lanterns hang from the ceiling, and deep reds bellow from the carpet, upholstered chairs, and walls. The Chinese decor prepares you for an authentic Chinese dining experience that includes a farm-to-table philosophy.

"My grandpa was beyond his time," says Bobby Tsui, a third-generation co-owner. Well before the farm-to-table movement, Eddie wanted fresh, local produce used in his kitchens. Rather than outsource agricultural duties, he purchased his own farm. There he grew jumbo spring onions, garlic sprouts, leeks, and cabbage. Although Eddie has passed away, the 133-acre farm remains in the family's possession, and twice a week, produce makes the ninety-minute journey to Peking Gourmet's kitchens.

The jumbo spring onions grow to about three feet high outside. But because sunlight changes the color and texture of garlic sprouts, the

Vintage Spot

Duangrat's Thai

Ed and Pookie Duangrat opened a small market in 1980 that supplied the Thai restaurant they opened seven years later. Crystal chandeliers hang from the ceilings, servers wear traditional Thai clothing, and paintings on the red walls celebrate Thai culture. When the restaurant opened, the kitchen Westernized its menu, but as Washingtonians have become increasingly adventurous and global, the menu has become increasingly authentic.

**5878 Leesburg Pike, Falls Church, VA 22041,
(703) 820-5775, duangrats.com**

sprouts grow inside a windowless barn. Peking Gourmet leaves the ducks up to another farmer in Pennsylvania, and each one weighs between 6 and 6.5 pounds.

While the Peking Gourmet Inn's signature dish is definitely worth its $42 price, a plethora of tasty options fill out the menu. Chief among them is the New Zealand baby lamb chops, served Peking style, a recipe from Eddie's son George. "My dad is the mastermind of the kitchen," says Bobby. Dense and flavorfully pan seared with a slight crispiness, they're unique, albeit one of the more expensive items for $30.

All noodle dishes are made in-house, and the four-season string beans are prepared with garlic, onions, and soy sauce. The fried Chinese leek dumplings are especially mouthwatering. "All our dumplings are literally Grandma's recipes," says Deborah Lee, Bobby's cousin and co-owner. "A lot of the sauces we try to do ourselves," she adds. The house-made garlic

sauce is one of the most popular. "People buy the garlic sauce like soup," Bobby reports.

If you have room for dessert, try the toffee apples, peaches, or bananas. Topped with sesame seeds, spun sugar, and toffee, any of these fruits come warm on the inside and crunchy on the outside. They're the perfect bite-size pairing for your after-dinner fortune cookie, which hopefully says you will go to bed full and happy.

Eddie passed the restaurant down to his children, George, Robert, Lily, and Nina. Robert and Nina cashed out in 2005. George's son Bobby and Lily's daughter Deborah run Peking Gourmet today. But neither had a direct route to the family business. As children, their grandfather put them to work on the farm and in the restaurant, but both pursued other careers. Deborah worked in the financial world, and Bobby served as a marine. He was thinking about going back to active duty after some project management work for the government but decided to take over the family business instead.

"George and Lily were going to sell the place if someone in the family didn't take over," he recalls. "I couldn't let what my grandfather created and what Lily and George had done . . . I couldn't let that go." But he couldn't

Vintage Spot
Kazan Restaurant

A *kazan* is a special chafing dish used to prepare dishes for Turkey's sultan. Whether you're a sultan or not, step into this family-run restaurant for authentic Turkish dishes. Open since 1980, Kazan Restaurant is best known for its *döner kebab*.

6813 Redmond Drive, McLean, VA 22101,
(703) 734-1960, kazanrestaurant.com

do it alone. "The plan was to go back to school," says Deborah, "and then he calls me up and asks 'What are you doing? For the rest of your life?'" Together the cousins took over daily operations at Peking Gourmet in 2013.

The Peking Gourmet Inn became well known from a surprising source: the Bush family.

Marvin Bush, the youngest child of George H. W. Bush, dined at Peking often. He and Eddie's son George became friendly and knew each other on a first-name basis. First name *only*. When Marvin told George he'd like to bring his father to Peking one day, George thought little of it. Little did he know, Marvin's father was the vice president of the United States.

The first time H. W. dined at Peking Gourmet, he had some trouble paying. The restaurant didn't accept his credit card.

"My mom had to walk over to the table and say 'I'm sorry, Mr. Vice President. We don't accept American Express.'" He paid by check. Fear not, American Express users: the very next day, George and Lily had American Express installed.

H. W.'s visit turned into fifty more. George Senior most likely cultivated his love of Chinese food while serving as chief of the U.S. Liaison Office to China under Gerald Ford. H. W.'s frequent visits to Peking Gourmet even led to the installation of a bulletproof glass window and put Peking Gourmet on the map.

The walls at Peking Gourmet tell the story of its other famous visitors, including Bill Clinton, Supreme Court Justice Sonia Sotomayor on the night she was sworn in, singer Psy, actor Robert Duvall, Janet Napolitano, and an entire wall of esteemed military personnel.

The restaurant was able to expand from its one room with just a few tables to several rooms seating about three hundred. If you're smart, you'll grab a table soon.

PORTOFINO

526 23RD STREET S • ARLINGTON, VA 22202

(703) 979-8200 • THEPORTOFINORESTAURANT.COM

VA Is for Lovers (of Lasagna)

The Micheli family has cooking in their blood. Three generations of Micheli family chefs built and sustain Portofino, a traditional Italian restaurant in Crystal City.

Adelmo Micheli operated a cafe in Italy, and his wife operated a cafe in Venezuela. They raised their son Sergio in Genoa, and he attended culinary school in Tuscany. Sergio came to the United States with the Italian navy and remained after his service ended in the 1960s. He worked as a chef at upscale Georgetown restaurant 1789. He convinced his father to join him in the United States, and Adelmo also landed a job at 1789. Sergio and Adelmo decided to go into business together and opened Portofino in 1970.

The next generation joined the father-son team: after attending the Culinary Institute of America (the *other* CIA), Sergio's son Richard became a partner at Portofino in 1992. He ran the restaurant with his wife, Pilar, and his sister, Maria Puletti.

Snake around Portofino to access the entrance in the back. After walking up a small set of stairs, enter the dimly lit front room, which gives way to a larger, sunnier veranda room. Plates with a black circumference and a curvy "P" for Portofino grace the tables, draped with diagonally layered pink and flowered tablecloths.

Light jazz plays overhead. A cappuccino machine from the 1950s serves as a sort of statue. Truly gigantic bottles of wine flank the machine on both sides. A red and yellow stained-glass window casts colored light on bottles

of vino in a wine closet. "It's not a family pizza place," says Richard. "On the other hand it's not über luxury." The Old World style of the restaurant is upscale without feeling stuffy, welcoming without feeling elementary. Various prints of seaport scenes grace the walls, a nod to the restaurant's namesake.

Portofino is a northwestern resort and fishing town on the Italian Riviera within the province of Genoa. Pastel houses line the pebbled beaches, and boats and yachts fill its harbors. Portofino has attracted the rich and famous for decades. Elizabeth Taylor and Richard Burton enjoyed the city years ago, while Beyoncé celebrated her thirty-third birthday in Portofino more recently.

Richard never expected to throw on his father's chef hat. "I didn't go to college with the expectation of being in the kitchen," he recalls. Instead he studied hotel and restaurant management at James Madison University. But while at JMU, a friend who had previously attended culinary school sparked Richard's desire to follow in his father and grandfather's footsteps.

As a teenager growing up in Portofino, Richard learned every job, from dishwasher to server. Now with culinary training under his belt, he knew the full spectrum of owning and managing a restaurant. "You understand what the employees have to deal with," he empathizes.

Portofino offers a combination of traditional Italian food and modern American entrees. The most popular item is the Bolognese lasagna. The family recipe for the chicken Portofino, a boneless chicken breast stuffed with prosciutto, spinach, and parmigiana cheese in a wine cream sauce, is also very popular, as is the veal-stuffed bococini. These small veal rolls are stuffed with mushroom and veal. The *omaggi di Nettuno,* a combination of lobster tail, shrimp, scallops, and mushrooms in brandy cream sauce served over fettuccine, is another top-selling family specialty.

When Portofino opened, DC had less variation than it does now. "[Restaurants were] either a family steak house or fine dining," says Richard. "Now there's so much in between."

Vintage Spot

ESSY'S CARRIAGE HOUSE

Since founder and chef Essy Saedi opened Essy's in 1975, the restaurant has brought white-tablecloth fine dining to Arlington. The upscale eatery is best known for its crab cakes, osso buco, and beef Stroganoff.

4030 Lee Highway, Arlington, VA 22207,
(703) 525-7899, essyscarriagehouse.com

As restaurants have become less and less formal, Portofino has become more casual. The restaurant once discouraged patrons without suit jackets from dining there, but that policy has waned over time. "I took my wife out to a very nice restaurant and there were people in shorts next to us," says Richard, remarking on the prevalence of casual attire. "We're gonna treat them as wonderfully as anybody," assures Richard. The staff has also gotten less formal. The waiters once wore tuxedos but have since abandoned the penguin look.

In the future, Richard says he may add a bar to Portofino to keep up with the competition. Thirty or forty years ago, "You went to a bar or you went to a restaurant," remembers Richard. But now "every restaurant that's opened in the last twenty years has a bar attached to it." Like Freddie Mercury, customers want it all.

Portofino's menu changes once a year, but have no fear: the classic Italian dishes like lasagna and veal Marsala aren't going anywhere. In January, Richard likes to look back on the previous year and analyze what's working and what's waning. "We take a couple off, put a couple on. Pare the menu in that sense," he says.

The clientele ranges from business professionals to young families, empty nesters, and retirees. With many hotels nearby, Portofino also serves plenty of business travelers. Some of the regulars are actually out-of-towners who make Portofino their go-to spot when working in DC.

In the future Richard expects Portofino to remain in the family, but "I'm not pushing it," he says of the next generation's involvement. No matter who runs Portofino, he plans for the restaurant to be around a long time. "We know we have good food," he says. And if a restaurant's been in business for forty-five years, it seems the public agrees.

THE PRIME RIB

2020 K STREET NW • WASHINGTON, DC 20006

(202) 466-8811 • THEPRIMERIB.COM

The Civilized Steak House

Four men in tuxedos greet you at the entrance to the Prime Rib. Their smiles belong to Clark Gable, Jimmy Stewart, Van Heflin, and Gary Cooper, the "Four Kings of Hollywood" at a 1957 New Year's Eve party. Dripping with old-school charm, the picture sets the tone for the fine dining experience inside. Here men still wear jackets to dinner, and women dress to the nines. Elegant black-and-white decor creates a 1940s vibe at this 1976 institution.

Brothers Buzz and Nick BeLer opened their first Prime Rib restaurant in 1965. "We were born and raised in the restaurant business," says Buzz. As young adults, Buzz put his law degree to use for a while, and Nick worked for the Food and Drug Administration. But the restaurant business remained of interest to the duo. They had always been close growing up and wanted to work together. Nick scouted a location in Baltimore, and they opened their first Prime Rib there in 1965.

"We both always wanted to open a restaurant in the nation's capital," says Buzz. Two days before our nation's bicentennial, DC's Prime Rib opened on July 2, 1976. "When we opened here, there were a number of really fine French restaurants," says Buzz. "We thought they could use a Prime restaurant. . . . We focused on beef and seafood [and] were able to compete."

The Prime Rib's signature dish is, predictably, its prime rib. The restaurant sells about four hundred pounds of prime rib a *day*. Carnivores will also enjoy its many meaty offerings, such as its rack of lamb, pork chops, steaks, and chicken piccata. The Prime Rib is also known for its fresh seafood. The restaurant receives daily deliveries from ports in Alaska, Maryland, and Denmark. Those deliveries bring softshell crabs, Chilean sea bass, and Maine lobster to your plate. Classic vegetable and potato sides complete a meat-lover's meal.

The decor is simple and elegant. A gigantic black-and-white vase of calla lilies serves as the nucleus of the space. It stands atop the center of four connected black leather booths, each like a petal on a flower. Napkins folded like swans rest at each table setting. Black chairs with a gold-button perimeter line the black bar. They go with the black walls, and leopard-print carpet alludes to the aggressive moves taken by men and women who can afford the Prime Rib's high prices.

In the "power room," play a game of "one of these things is not like the other." The outlier is a chair at each table that is more of a throne than a chair. Here you can "hold court" with your subordinates, Buzz jokes.

Sketches by Louis Icart featuring various female nudes hang throughout the restaurant. My favorite is *Cigarette*, which depicts a blonde woman seamlessly taking shape in the smoke rising from a cigarette. A gigantic print of famous French drag cabaret performer Alice Soulie by Jean-Gabriel Domergue also hangs near the kitchen.

A baby grand piano sits near the bar. You can hear live piano and bass every evening. It's the kind of place where Frank Sinatra would (and has) crooned into the night. The Prime Rib's current bass player accompanied Sinatra at the White House with the Marine Band. One night, famous jazz singer Diana Krall treated dinner guests to an impromptu set of tunes, and on another, Muhammad Ali sat down at the piano. You can't count on that happening during your visit, but the Prime Rib is the kind of place it *could*.

The Prime Rib has remained consistent while DC has changed around it. Buzz identifies this consistency as a big part of Prime's success. "You come here and you know what you're going to get," he explains. With new, flashy restaurants taking over the increasingly foodie culture of DC, the Prime Rib has faced more competition over the years. "Of course, the competition has grown as the restaurant business in this town has really blossomed," says Buzz. But the success of AMC's *Mad Men* has actually made some diners more likely to step foot inside the Prime Rib, perhaps wearing outfits from Banana Republic's *Mad Men* collection. For diners craving a throwback to classier times, tables at the Prime Rib are available.

Powerful clientele matches the Prime Rib's atmosphere. Buzz counts politicians, admirals, generals, and movie actors among his typical customers. The space has a definite male energy. (Male Hollywood movie stars greet you as you enter, and naked women adorn the walls.) Catering to big-time players in politics and finance has historically drawn men through the door. But as our economic and political landscapes become more equal among the sexes, that may change. Famous customers to date have included Liberace and Arnold Schwarzenegger. Schwarzenegger forgot to wear a jacket when he visited the Prime Rib, and the jacket offered him wouldn't fit over his large muscles, so the restaurant dropped its dinner jacket requirement for the buff star.

Buzz opened a third Prime Rib in Philadelphia. Unfortunately, he had to do it solo, as Nick passed away in 1995. Buzz's son works with him, keeping the family's work in the restaurant industry alive. The Food Network's *Meat Men* called Buzz "the Godfather of Steak in Washington, DC." Fitting for a man who will make you an offer you can't refuse: the Prime Rib.

QUILL

AT THE JEFFERSON HOTEL

1200 16TH STREET NW • WASHINGTON, DC 20036

(202) 448-2300 • JEFFERSON.COM/DINING/QUILL

All Things Jefferson

Thomas Jefferson loved books and wine. At the Jefferson, you can indulge in both. A hotel that celebrates our third president, the Jefferson contains a book room and bar named Quill that espouses Jefferson's favorite things.

Quill's parquet flooring takes its cue from Jefferson's Monticello salon. Decor in brown and gold gives the small, two-room space a refined, serious vibe. The first room contains a grand piano before an elegant set of circular golden mirrors and six tables with sprawling chairs. Most nights, pianist Peter Robinson treats guests to music at 9 p.m. Maps charting Jefferson's travels through Europe give a history lesson on the walls.

While serving as minister (ambassador) to France from 1785 to 1789, Jefferson traveled extensively throughout France, Germany, and Italy. In addition to being one of our nation's most influential founding fathers, Jefferson was a farmer. "He said his favorite job was as a farmer," says Joan Esposito, the Jefferson's director of sales and history buff. A man of the soil, Jefferson had a great interest in food and beverage, specifically wine. Jefferson's travels allowed him to explore some of Europe's finest wineries.

The second room that makes up Quill contains its luminous orange-hued bar. Sturdy, seat-backed stools provide seating at the bar and high tables. Drawings of founding fathers John Quincy Adams, James Madison, Ben Franklin, James Monroe, and John Adams hang on the walls. In the right corner, an early design of the Washington Monument reveals what the landmark might have looked like if architect Rob Mills's original design had been realized.

Mills's winning design in an 1833 contest had an Egyptian obelisk emerging from the roof of a circular structure with thirty columns. A statue of George Washington riding a chariot topped the sphere. However, the Washington National Monument Society scrapped Mills's base and went with the simple obelisk you can see from all over the city today.

A bevy of European wines appear on Quill's menu from regions such as Burgundy, Mosel, Kamptal, and Umbria. A trio of seasonal cocktails is available, along with a mocktail named the Monticello that combines seasonal berries with sage and lavender-infused honey.

The menu is as American as the man who inspired the bar. Sides like macaroni and cheese, mashed potatoes, and brussels sprouts roasted with bacon can accompany any of the meat and fish entrees. Small bites on the appetizer menu offer the most diversity. They include pulled pork sliders, lobster bisque, crab cakes, and salmon tartare.

Expect to be waited on with great attention and service: the Jefferson has a 2:1 employee-to-guest ratio. On a winter afternoon, one guest asks for a magnifying glass and is presented with one less than a minute later. President Obama has visited Quill, located just a few blocks from the White House, "on more than one occasion," says Esposito. The clientele regularly includes Capitol Hill workers, figures in the entertainment industry, and out-of-town guests.

After enjoying a beverage and comparing your passport stamps to Jefferson's at Quill, pop into the book room. It's a small space that pays tribute to Jefferson's love of reading. "He literally did say to John Adams, 'I cannot live without books,'" relays Esposito. "Jefferson also liked the smaller, intimate places" at his estate, Esposito elaborates. He most certainly would have liked this one: a reader can settle into a chair by the fireplace surrounded by books or draw the curtains in a private booth to escape into a world of nonfiction or fantasy. "We Google all our guests and put their books in the book room," reveals Esposito. (Perhaps you're reading *this* book in the book room right now.)

You might spy the hotel's resident beagle, Lord Monticello, while at the Jefferson, a canine replication of Jefferson's life. Jefferson brought a French sheepdog named Bergère and her two puppies to the United States in 1789. However, he had a tempestuous relationship with the species. The farmer exemplified great hostility toward dogs that ate or ruined his sheep. In 1808, he instructed his overseer, "To secure wool enough, the Negroes' dogs must all be killed. Do not spare a single one." And in a letter to a friend in 1811, Jefferson wrote, "I participate in all your hostility to dogs and would readily join in any plan of exterminating the whole race." Mitt Romney was vilified for threatening Big Bird's life in a 2012 presidential election debate. Imagine what the Internet would have done to Jefferson if his disdain for dogs had today's levels of exposure. (Admittedly a distant evil to being a slave owner . . .)

If you're in the mood for a more expensive, five-star-dining experience, head for the Jefferson's other restaurant, Plume. The menu draws inspiration from Thomas Jefferson's Monticello harvests.

And before leaving the Jefferson, take a good look at the documents framed on the walls of the lobby. They're all various treaties and documents signed by Jefferson through the years.

The Jefferson Hotel dates back to 1923, when it was known as the Jefferson Apartments. French architect Jules Henri de Sibour named his buildings in presidential order: his first was named for Washington, his second for Adams, and his third for Jefferson. Jules's résumé includes the French embassy, Peruvian embassy, the Uzbekistan embassy, and the original Folger Theater. Before technology made commuting between home states and Washington, DC, easy, many politicians resided at the Jefferson Apartments. In 1955, the apartments were converted into the Jefferson Hotel, and in 2007, the hotel closed for two years to undergo an extreme makeover.

History buffs should take a cue from Thomas Jefferson's penchant for exploration and investigate all the Jefferson has to offer.

THE RAVEN GRILL

3125 MT. PLEASANT STREET NW, #101 • WASHINGTON, DC 20010

(202) 387-8411

Dive In

"On my second shift here, this guy came in smoking a cigar. I said, 'Hey, man, you can't smoke in here.' He turned around and started punching me [then] tries to burn out a guy with a lit cigar."

Tariq Haqq has been a bartender at the Raven Grill for five years, and while many people would recount that story with horror, he tells it as an example of why this is "the coolest bar I've ever worked in." Haqq's childhood expectations of what it would be like to work in a bar are coming true. "Uncommon problems are common here," he says. His no-frills, tell-it-like-it-is attitude fits perfectly with the Raven, a dive bar that's known for its concise offerings and lack of kitchen, despite the "grill" in its name.

Open since 1935, the Raven Grill was family owned for many years until current owner Merid Admassu purchased the bar. The Raven boasts DC's oldest liquor license, and not much has changed since its early days.

Twinkly lights decorate an exposed pipe that runs along the ceiling. A jukebox plays Stevie Wonder. Framed portraits of icons like Marilyn Monroe, Miles Davis, Bob Marley, and Elvis hang in the bar's six booths, lit by alternating green and yellow lamps.

Frank Sinatra's mug shot hangs on the opposite wall, along with a framed copy of the Declaration of Independence and the famous print *Nighthawks* (aka *Boulevard of Broken Dreams*) by Edward Hopper, depicting late-night diner goers.

The walls are a mixture of brick and wood, and some walls are artfully ink-blotted. A small area in the back plays an old black-and-white movie.

The bar itself is small, fitting about fifteen patrons hunched closely together. Even though there's a neon picture of a martini glass labeled "Cocktails" in the window, don't come here for a cocktail. It's not that kind of place. "We don't have Sprite here," says Haqq. Sprite would be too fancy for the Raven. Stick to beer or bourbon.

An orange water cooler perches on the bar near rows of Cheetos, Wheat Thins, and potato chips hanging on the wall. That's the only grub for sale. The Raven did serve food in its early days. A grill in the back churned out cheeseburgers and pickled eggs for fifteen cents. But those days are long gone.

A trio of board games peeks out from behind an ATM: Scrabble, Password, and You Might Be a Redneck If . . .

A small chalkboard above the bar scribbles:

George's Twitter:

"I have more scars than brain cells."

Who is George? In a place like this, he could be the guy who wasn't too pleased about the no-smoking rule communicated by Haqq.

The Raven is the kind of place that wouldn't have a website, and doesn't. I'm surprised they even have a Facebook page.

The Raven Grill is a well-known watering hole on the border between Mount Pleasant and Columbia Heights. Mount Pleasant became a popular "streetcar suburb" of DC in the early twentieth century. In the 1960s, many immigrants, artists, and activists settled in the neighborhood. It earned the nickname "little UN" thanks to its Latino, Czech, and African-American populations. After the Czech Communist coup in 1948, Mount Pleasant gained Czech transplants, including an exiled four-star general and a Czech ambassador to Turkey. Today Mount Pleasant is known for its vibrant Dominican and El Salvadoran communities.

You may notice the streets in Mount Pleasant wind a little differently than the rest of the city. In 1791, the capital's architect, Pierre L'Enfant, designed DC with streets in a grid and diagonal avenues, but Mount Pleasant ignored these instructions. Instead, settlers with a case of *stickitothemanitis* continued to use existing farm roads or create roads based on natural land patterns.

The Raven Grill is a short quarter-mile walk from the Columbia Heights Metro station. Columbia Heights has enjoyed great development in the last sixteen years since the Metro opened in 1999.

Even though it has almost a hundred years of history, the Raven Grill doesn't seem to want anyone to know it. The Grill is listed on dozens of historic-bar lists and many "Things to Do in Mount Pleasant" lists, but nobody has any details. Sadly, neither do I. Repeated calls went unreturned to the elusive GM and owner, but maybe that's for the best. The Raven Grill wants to stay under the radar. If this place was packed with twentysomethings who thought it was the cool new place to be, it wouldn't be the Raven. Maybe whatever happened here in 1935 is meant to be remembered by the people who were actually there. If Harry Truman got drunk and sang the national anthem at the Raven in a high falsetto voice, there wouldn't be a plaque commemorating the story. There'd be people who passed the story down to enjoy among themselves.

One woman who took years of this place's stories to her grave was the brash and beloved Mary T. Gregory, a bartender who died in 2011 at the age of eighty-four, just six years after retiring from a forty-three-year career at the Raven Grill.

If you're not hungry but you're in the mood for a cheap beer in a pretension-free environment, travel Mount Pleasant's off-kilter streets to the Raven Grill.

The First Farm to Table

*B*eing green was once, well, green. Before farmers' markets were commonplace, before Whole Foods, before eating organic was as trendy as the latest iPhone, there was Restaurant Nora. Opened in 1979 by Nora Pouillon, Restaurant Nora is the nation's first certified organic restaurant.

Austrian immigrant Nora noticed Americans' unhealthy eating habits when she moved to the United States in 1965. Her passion for cooking at home bloomed into an early career as a cooking teacher and caterer. Nora developed relationships with organic farmers in neighboring states, using their ingredients in her cooking classes and catering jobs.

When she became the executive chef at the Tabard Inn, Nora became a true professional chef. She also found love with her second husband, Steven Damato, the Tabard Inn's manager.

With Steven and his brother Thomas, Nora opened Restaurant Nora in 1979. The restaurant brought Nora's passions for healthy food and environmentalism to life. In addition to serving organic food, Restaurant Nora uses wind power, prints its menus on recycled paper, composts its waste, and washes its linens in an eco-friendly manner.

Nora recognized that even Americans who *thought* they ordered healthy meals were getting more calories than expected. "In main courses, I didn't want to have any hidden calories," says Nora. "I cook with sunflower oil or olive oil," she says, refusing to "tarnish" healthy dishes like salmon with fatty oils and butter. "I use plenty of butter, sugar, and cream in my desserts, but then you know what you're getting."

For diners with dietary restrictions, Restaurant Nora is a transparent safe haven. "I have people coming here, saying this is the only restaurant I can bring my son to because he's allergic to everything under the sun," says Nora. Dietary restrictions aren't an annoyance at Restaurant Nora. They're accommodated.

Nora worked to expand organic living beyond her restaurant. She helped create DC's FRESHFARM Markets and organized bus tours connecting DC chefs with organic farmers. She also teamed with certifying agency Oregon Tilth to create a set of criteria to certify restaurants as organic. In 1999, Restaurant Nora became the first eatery to receive this distinction. Relatively few have followed in her footsteps. Many restaurants simply don't want to limit themselves to organic ingredients. "It limits their creativity, so they say," explains Nora.

Nora estimates her menu changes by about 20 percent on a daily basis, depending on what's available from her farmers. Patrons can enjoy a tasting menu or items à la carte. A tasting menu might begin with a roasted red pepper soup, followed by multigrain risotto with mushrooms, leeks, spinach, parmesan tuile, and herb salad, finished off with a bittersweet molten chocolate cake topped with cappuccino ice cream.

The à la carte menu features small plates like the Maine peekytoe crab and avocado salad flavored with chili, tortillas, and cilantro. Main dishes range from scallops and salmon to lamb shanks and strip steak, all seasoned with a bevy of vegetables and spices.

The restaurant's clientele has grown increasingly educated over the years. "At the beginning, when I opened up, I said 'organic restaurant,' and they said, 'What is this, a biology class?'" jokes Nora. Patrons failed to connect the rich flavors and great taste of their food with its method of preparation. Now Nora's customers not only make the connection, they seek it out.

Restaurant Nora has served several presidents over the years, but perhaps the most appropriate guest has been Michelle Obama. Nora's exemplifies Mrs. Obama's mission to promote healthy eating and curb childhood obesity.

However, Nora doesn't think that efforts from the top down will fix Americans' health crisis. She insists it must come from the average American, from the bottom up. "There has to be a sort of uproar about demanding healthy food," she says. "It's going in the right direction. I just don't know if we are moving fast enough to avoid a terrible sort of disaster in the next thirty, fifty years."

Nora decorated her restaurant with geometric patterned Mennonite and Amish crib quilts. The Mennonite and Amish communities' connection to the soil exemplifies the restaurant's mission. Several art pieces, like a 1940s model plane, also hang from the ceiling, and fan windows and other artifacts hang on the red-and-white-painted brick walls.

The main dining room, which seats about eighty, once housed the delivery horses of the grocery store that occupied the property a century ago. Jutting off the main room, the Garden Room boasts great lighting from slated ceiling windows, a bed of roses, and painted farm scenes. The Wine Room is intimate but feels bigger, thanks to an optical illusion from two wine bottles reflected in a set of mirrors.

Nora has introduced an organic lifestyle to DC, but she has bigger plans: a chain restaurant on par with McDonald's that offers low-cost, fast organic food. Many argue that poor people cannot afford to buy organic. But in the long run, Nora doesn't think it costs more. "I always say I prefer to spend the money on food than on my doctor," she explains. Time will tell if she can pull it off.

For now, she's focused on Restaurant Nora, where she believes promoting a healthy, sustainable lifestyle promotes peace. When eating the meat of an abused animal, Nora argues, "You eat a little bit of that emotion from that animal." Consuming violence creates violence. "I truly believe [human violence] has a lot to do with the food we eat." But by serving meat from well-treated animals and fairly compensated, free workers, Nora's approach to food benefits more than your waistline.

Nora hopes her customers exit feeling better than when they entered. And if the restaurant's approach to healthy living influences customers' habits at home, even better.

ROUND ROBIN BAR

AT THE WILLARD INTERCONTINENTAL

1401 PENNSYLVANIA AVENUE NW • WASHINGTON, DC 20004

(202) 628-9100 • WASHINGTON.INTERCONTINENTAL.COM

Bipartisan Potions

*J*f you want to drink like a president, set your compass for the Round Robin Bar in the Willard InterContinental Hotel. A block from the White House, this intimate power bar has served commanders in chief since 1850.

Enter through the lavish lobby where the term "lobbyist" was coined during the Grant administration, when favor-seeking politicos who interrupted the president while he enjoyed a cigar or beverage were nicknamed "lobbyists." Be sure to look up, where every state's seal is beautifully engraved on the ceiling.

Make a right off the lobby to enter the Round Robin. Portraits of presidents and writers who threw back at the Robin hang on the dark-green walls. But the focus of the Round Robin is its sophisticated circular bar.

This bar's name has nothing to do with birds. Rather, "round robin" comes from the French phrase *rond ribbon,* a round ribbon. Disgruntled French peasants signed their names to petitions demanding change in the 1600s and 1700s. To crush opposition, the king frequently beheaded the first people listed, reasoning that they were the instigators. Some Frenchmen got the bright idea to sign their names in a circular pattern, like a ribbon, so that every name bore equal weight. Plus, it would be much harder to behead them all.

Today the term "round robin" celebrates this idea of equal status. In round robin sport tournaments, every team plays each other. At a round robin dance, everyone boogies with each other. The circular bar at the Round Robin reflects this ideology. Straightened out, the bar would stretch about fifty feet, and conversation would be limited to those on a customer's left and right. But a circular bar promotes an equal exchange of ideas, a fitting structure for its history of catering to those elected to represent this country's diverse population.

This respect for all points of view dates back to the Civil War, when the Willard was a neutral ground in DC. However, visitors could indicate their Northern or Southern allegiances based on which door they chose to enter the hotel. Today fear not: the entrance you choose reflects nothing about your politics.

The Round Robin features seasonal drinks inspired by DC's political and seasonal climate.

In the winter, you can enjoy a piping hot William Henry Harrison Spiced Cider, named for President Harrison, who often drank cider with an egg in the morning to settle his stomach. In the spring, cocktails inspired by DC's blooming cherry blossoms are available, and in January, the Round Robin features its famous POTUS-inspired drink menu in honor of the State of the Union Address.

Jim Hewes, the Round Robin's famous mixologist, has concocted a cocktail for each man to hold the Oval Office. When creating a cocktail, Hewes tries to blend taste with history. "It's one thing to just have a good cocktail," says Hewes, "but people love a story."

The Round Robin's Orange Blossom, for example, has sneaky origins: When Rutherford B. Hayes took office in 1877, his wife, Lucy, barred alcohol from the White House. But the press bribed servers to spike the beverages, inspiring the Round Robin's Orange Blossom, a not-so-covert mix of gin and orange juice.

The Round Robin welcomed Barack Obama into office with the Blue Hawaiian: a drink blending tequila, curaçao, and lime juice to create a blue cocktail, alluding to our forty-fourth president's island state. George W. Bush, who quit drinking at forty, is commemorated with a simple Diet Coke and lemon.

Feel free to ask for the Presidential Cocktail Menu at any time of the year. Bound in an important-looking black binder, the book features all forty-four drinks. James Madison is honored with French champagne thanks to his wife, who loved "all things Fine, Fashionable, and French," and Ulysses S. Grant is commemorated with Roman Punch. According to the menu, it was so cold at Grant's inaugural ball that this champagne-and-fruit concoction froze in the punch bowls.

If you want to step down the chain of command from president to secretary of state, order a mint julep. Henry Clay is most famous for spearheading the Compromise of 1850, but he is also the father of the modern mint julep. Rumor has it that after Clay asked to substitute bourbon for the customary cognac in his drink at the Round Robin, we've been drinking it that way ever since. Other than Louisville on Kentucky Derby weekend, Hewes says, "We probably make more mint juleps than anywhere in the country."

The Round Robin's food menu reflects the Willard's intent to serve premium items that are classic yet trendy. The meatball starters are made with veal or pork, and the macaroni and cheese is specialized with truffle oil, Gruyère, and prosciutto. The menu offers sliders, burgers, and salads that are great for individuals or for sharing.

The Round Robin's refined decor will make you feel powerful by proxy, and the gaslight-inspired lamps will transport you to a simpler time. Enjoying a meal or sipping on a soda, you can appreciate the history of the bar and its host hotel, where Martin Luther King Jr. stayed on the eve of his "I Have a Dream" speech and where Abraham Lincoln laid his head the night before his inauguration.

"What's different about the bar scene in DC," explains Hewes, is that "you go to a [DC] bar to find out what's going to be on the front page tomorrow." Sitting at the Round Robin's circular mahogany bar, you might find out, as the bar often serves government employees visiting DC to advocate for their hometowns. Hewes has served heads of state, senators, and congressmen and has carded famous authors, artists, and actors. There's no guarantee you'll bump into anyone shaping the nation's policy or culture, but if you're looking for a historical place to socialize, this is it.

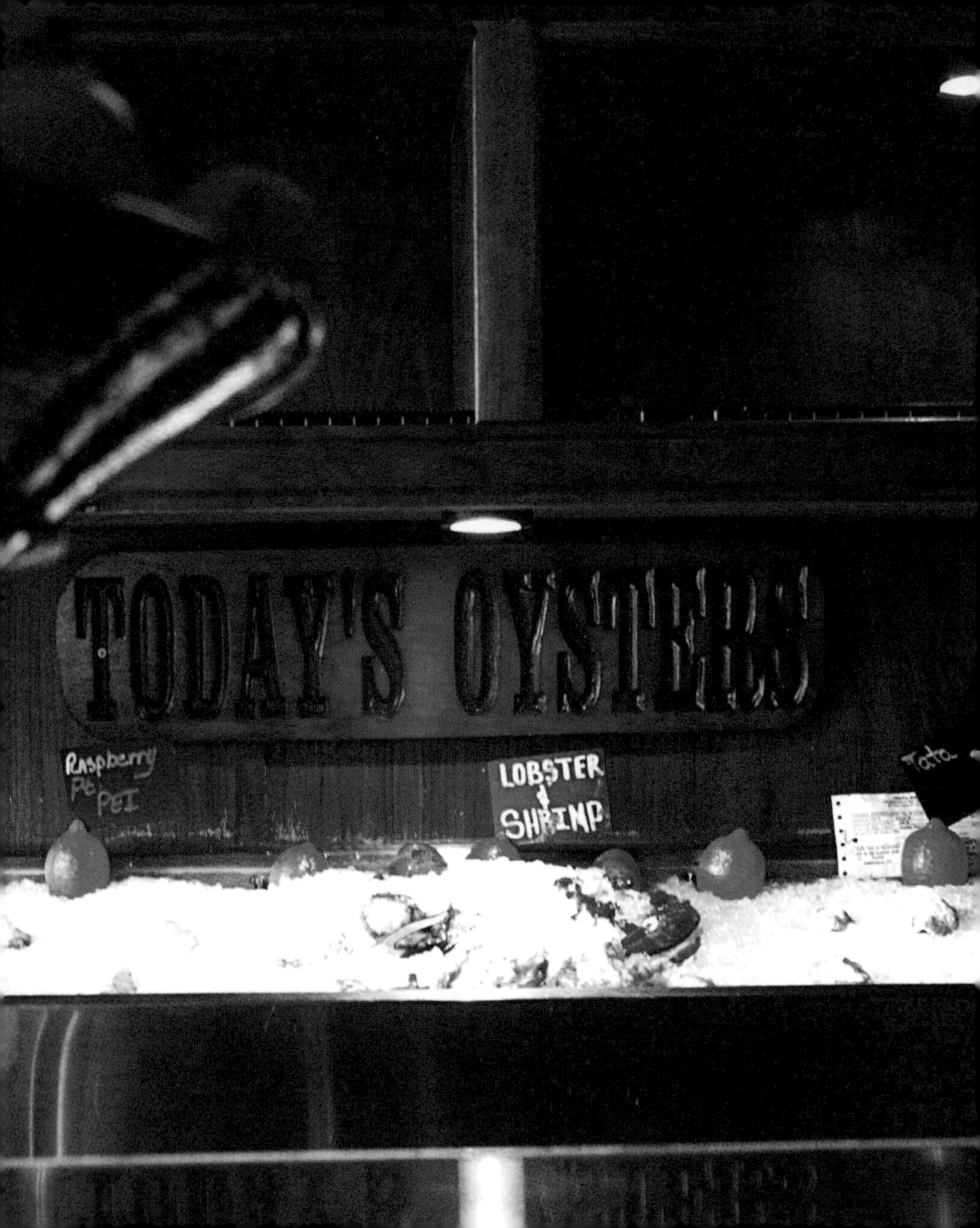
TODAY'S OYSTERS
Raspberry
PEI
LOBSTER & SHRIMP

SENART'S OYSTER & CHOP HOUSE

520 8TH STREET SE • WASHINGTON, DC 20003

(202) 544-1168 • SENARTSDC.COM

Oysters from Ashes

Sometimes things come back from the dead. Jesus is the most obvious example, and fashion provides plenty of examples, but in 2011, an oyster and chop house that operated from 1913 to 1939 was resurrected on Barracks Row.

The Senart family ran the original Oyster & Chop House. They lived above the restaurant in a one-bedroom apartment. Founder Xavier Cervera decided to breathe new life into the old restaurant. Cervera restored a fading one-hundred-year-old Coca-Cola "ghost mural" on the side of the honey-and-chocolate-colored exterior that feels like a structure you'd find off the water in coastal Maine. Cervera oversaw the restoration, decor, and opening of Senart's until selling it in 2012.

Inside, Senart's decor exemplifies the old-meets-new that is its story. A large painting of a real fight that took place outside Senart's hangs on the wall near the entrance. The cobblestone roads and newsboy caps worn by the painting's subjects place the scene in the restaurant's early days of operation. A fifty-foot-long Italian Carrera marble slab bar provides a view for "Today's Oysters" on display in a bed of ice and lemon. On any given day, those oysters might hail from ports in Virginia, Maryland, Delaware, Pennsylvania, and more. Walnut bar stools, tables, and black leather banquettes emulate the style in effect at the original Senart's a century ago.

Political cartoons and snapshots of DC monuments root Senart's in its city. The walls feature black-and-white work by famed photojournalist A.

Aubrey Bodine, who chronicled regional life for fifty years with the *Baltimore Sun*.

A few tables provide outdoor seating surrounded by attractive flowerbeds in the spring and summer.

Obviously, Senart's specializes in oysters and chops.

Two oyster dishes may catch your eye: the oysters Rockefeller pairs hand-shucked oysters with bacon, creamed spinach, and Gruyère. And the fried oyster sandwich places oysters, bacon, lettuce, tomato, pickle, and aioli between slices of ciabatta. Of course, you can pick from the daily selection of oysters by the half or full dozen. During happy hour, from 3 to 7 p.m. every day, oysters cost only $1 each.

On the "chops" side of its name, Senart's highlights a hanger steak in a Bordelaise sauce that comes with buttermilk-soaked onion rings and baby carrots. The menu also features a double-cut pork chop that brilliantly pairs creamy polenta with brussels sprouts, bacon, caramelized onion, and mustard.

Executive chef Brendan Tharp's menu also includes a braised Colorado lamb shank, a beef short rib, a pan-seared duck in a port-wine reduction, and a half grilled chicken with collard greens and mashed potatoes.

If you don't wake up yearning for a steak or an oyster, Senart's also serves brunch. Fifteen-dollar bottomless mimosas pair well with the crab and prosciutto eggs Benedict or the french toast with candied bacon, maple butter, and fruit.

The menu features only two desserts, a cinnamon, vanilla, and candied bacon bread pudding and a classic cheesecake. But if you take advantage of starters like a cheese plate or french fries dressed up with foie gras and cheese curds, you won't even ask for a dessert menu after your entree.

After oysters and chops, Senart's should be known for its cocktails. "Good drinks is what we do," says bartender Lance Smith, who claims he makes "a perfect Manhattan" and likes to concoct drinks tailored to his customers. "They're fostering creativity behind the bar," approves general manager Mike. "If you don't see it on the menu, just ask for it, and we'll make it happen." Smith says champagne cocktails sell particularly well at Senart's, and Mike adds, "People love their whiskeys here." And they have plenty to choose from: the bar stocks about twenty different bourbons in addition to a long list of single-malt Scotches and sparkling, red, and white wines.

The neighborhood has the charm of a small town, but that is a relatively recent development. In the 1800s, Barracks Row pulsed as the heartbeat of DC's economy. Minutes from the Navy Yard, Barracks Row thrived. But after World War II, when navy jobs fizzled and residents moved to the suburbs, the neighborhood declined. The former commercial hub declined further after the 1968 riots when businesses burned and the neighborhood developed a seedy reputation. But a revitalization movement took shape in the 1990s and 2000s, and its success has made Barracks Row a destination for dining and commerce once again. With a plethora of restaurants and beautification efforts, the neighborhood has become simultaneously cutting edge and charming.

After enjoying a meal at Senart's, look around the neighborhood for a group of one-story "shotgun" houses, named for their parallel front and rear doors. A bullet shot through the front door could exit through the back door. And look for the Old Naval Hospital at 9th and Pennsylvania SE. This hospital housed Confederate soldiers taken prisoner during the Civil War. And don't forget to walk south and take a peek at the Navy Yard or stroll along the water.

Senart's enjoys a navy presence, and has even served the marine corps commandant since reopening. The bar gets its fair share of important political figures, but "people leave that at their jobs," says Smith. "[They] come in and talk about life." In between slurps and bites, of course.

The reincarnation of Senart's Oyster & Chop House fits perfectly into a historic neighborhood making its own comeback.

STETSON'S

1610 U STREET NW • WASHINGTON, DC 20009

(202) 667-6295 • STETSONS-DC.COM

Booze by Bootleggers

Jf the walls at Stetson's could talk, they'd tell stories of secret drinking during Prohibition and beers being poured here since 1904. The two-floored bar wears its age, but as hits from Taylor Swift and Maroon 5 play back-to-back on a Saturday night, old meets new.

Before Prohibition, the space housed the John Morris Saloon and then a bar called McCarthy's. Afterward, it became a speakeasy during the years of banned alcohol consumption.

During the 1960s, the space became Alfred's Steak House and then a Tex-Mex restaurant called Mr. J's. The bullet holes you can find in the ceiling and window of Stetson's are there courtesy of Mr. J, a retired Secret Service officer, and his drinking buddies, who used to get drunk and fire their weapons after hours inside.

After the 1968 riots, the neighborhood struggled to attract crowds. "All of this was a no-man's land," says Stetson's assistant general manager Tommy Osborne. "All the businesses had left." In 1980, retired police officer Tommy Keeley purchased Mr. J's and renamed it Stetson's. He kept the bullhorns and cowboy hats on the wall out of respect for Mr. J. But don't expect to see anybody in a cowboy hat looking for a mechanical bull. The wall decor and a few menu items is where the Tex-Mex homage stops.

If it's too crowded at the first floor's long bar, take the black-and-red staircase up to a game room that features an AC/DC pinball machine, a Big Buck shooting game, a pool table, foosball, and two dartboards. A

"Landshark" surfboard with a large bite taken out of it hangs on the ceiling above the room's bar. Murphy's, Budweiser, and Miller High Life are just a few of the beer logos adorning the walls.

The patio outside feels like the backyard of the college house where you played beer pong on spring nights. Vines grow up the faded white brick of the building, and horizontal beams and latticework covered in twigs and shrubbery enclose the patio. Vertical wood panels join together to make a high exit gate much like the one Tom Sawyer had to paint. If he were here, he'd turn the job into a drinking game. Take a seat on plastic patio furniture or at a picnic table under a Sam Adams or Peroni umbrella.

The whiskey murals on the brick walls have dry origins: the Mojave Desert and Prohibition, to be exact. There were urban legends that Stetson's had been a speakeasy during Prohibition, but one day in 2005 while cleaning out the basement, Osborne found an old bottle of whiskey with Stetson's address marked from 1914. He thought, "Wow, the urban legends are true! This is for real!"

Six years later, a couple vacationing in the Mojave Desert saw something sticking out of the sand. It was an old bottle of John Morris Whiskey. "They recognized the address," says Osborne. "'Our son drinks there!'" How the bottle ended up in the Mojave Desert remains a mystery.

The couple mailed the whiskey bottle to Stetson's, and the managers put it in a case. "It was kind of our bar's sacred relic," says Osborne. "The general manager and I were the only ones who were allowed to touch it."

But when Tommy commissioned artist Chad Brady to paint murals of both whiskey bottles on the walls of the beer garden, the bottle found its way into Brady's clumsy hands. "He broke it after holding it for thirty seconds," relays Osborne. "He said, 'I'll give you a discount on the mural.' I said, 'Damn right you will.'" Osborne praises Chad's work as an artist but warns, "Don't trust him with anything breakable."

If you like trivia, come to Stetson's on Tuesday nights at 7 p.m. "We get some very serious players in here," says Osborne. Stetson's offers $9

Vintage Spot

Madam's Organ

Play with the words Adams Morgan and you get Madam's Organ, a blues bar and soul food restaurant that's been open for more than twenty years. The place is well known for its large, controversial mural of a redheaded woman with enormous bare breasts on the side of the building. The club features live blues and bluegrass nightly.

2461 18th Street NW, Washington, DC 20009,
(202) 667-5370, madamsorgan.com

Rolling Rock pitchers and a prize of $60 off the tab to the winning team. Pub quizmaster Mehun Etabara won $128,000 on *Jeopardy*, so you know you're in good hands. By day Etabara works for a think tank, and by night he devises eight categories of ten questions each for Stetson's brightest and dimmest.

Every two to four years, a new crop of college students and federal workers come and go, adding a fresh group of customers to Stetson's core clientele of down-to-earth neighborhood regulars. As DC's restaurant industry gets sleeker and sleeker, Stetson's doesn't try to keep up. "We kind of try to be the opposite of what a lot of places are," says Osborne. "It's just a place to come and be comfortable and hang out."

That relaxed vibe has attracted plenty of high-profile guests who want a break from stuffy, high-stakes environments. The bar became popular with the Democratic Party some years ago. "A lot of the bigwigs would come in here," says Osborne. "I don't want to name any names." But he does name two: Jenna and Barbara Bush. According to Osborne, the Bush twins threw drinks back at Stetson's before they were twenty-one. The bar hired a front-of-house bouncer after that.

The bar's menu serves some Tex-Mex food such as chips and salsa, nachos, and a quesadilla. But the majority of the menu is comfort American food, from chili cheese french fries to a number of burgers.

Stetson's small, outgoing staff of twelve likes to foster personal relationships with its guests. "We're not just get-you-in-get-you-out," says Osborne. "It's a 'come hang out in my living room' atmosphere. 'I've got games.'"

On a Roll Since 1976

*I*n the States, bigger is better. We supersize our orders and have memberships at Costco. But in Japan, less is more. The concept of "MA," meaning "the space between," influences many areas of Japanese culture, from the negative space in artwork, to rock gardens, ikebana, and food. At Sushiko, DC's first sushi restaurant, dating back to 1976, creative director Daisukye Utagawa has employed MA with what he calls a "cuisine of subtraction."

"One of the factors that's unique to Japan is this idea of editing," he says. "Subtracting things to show beauty." Utagawa wondered, "If I don't have soy, rice, [and] seaweed, can I still make Japanese food?" What was more important: ingredients or philosophy? By "subtracting" certain Japanese imports in favor of local ingredients like sea trout from the Chesapeake Bay and softshell crab, Utagawa got his answer. With a Japanese philosophy, these local ingredients could be used to prepare great Japanese cuisine. "Craft is important, but if you become a prisoner of craft, you don't go forward," he argues. At Sushiko, Utagawa wants to move forward.

A Japanese native, Utagawa spent a few years in DC as a child while his father worked as a journalist, and wanted to return. "I was led to believe that if I became a sushi chef, it would be easier [to get a green card]," he recalls. And so he joined Sushiko as a sushi chef in 1983, then located in Glover Park. Five years later, Utagawa took over. He was just twenty-four.

Sushiko's clientele has changed dramatically over the years. Today people from all walks of life dine in the stylish eatery. But in the beginning,

Japanese businessmen kept the restaurant afloat with their large expense accounts. The restaurant also catered to the Japanese embassy and Japanese locals craving a taste of home. Americans, still clinging to meats and heavy sauces, were not yet interested in raw fish.

But as purse strings tightened and expense accounts faded, sushi had been quietly making a play for palates since a Little Tokyo sushi restaurant started serving raw fish in Los Angeles.

By the 1980s, sushi had become wildly popular in the United States with a "roll craze." Utagawa refers to the former fad as "the bastardization of sushi," but admits, "It completely expanded the base of people who would eat sushi."

Sushiko's sushi chefs are not Japanese. "I'm quite proud of that," says Utagawa. "I've always believed that what makes chefs good is not their nationality but their passion and skills." Indonesian brothers Piter and Handry Tjan work as joint executive chefs at Sushiko, and their sushi offerings bring in Sushiko's main source of revenue. The Sweet and Spicy Roll combines eel, pickled ginger, spicy tuna, avocado, jalapeño, and kabayaki. The Softshell Crab Roll combines avocado, scallion, and spicy sesame sauce. For vegetarians, the East-West Roll teams sun-dried tomato, shiso, avocado, cucumber, and rice in soy paper, and is out of this world, especially when mixed with ponzu sauce and green tea salt. The roasted duck is very tender. It has a slight crispness on the perimeter of its brown and purple hues and is just shy of spicy after being marinated in soy, honey, and miso mustard. Japanese staples like chicken teriyaki and miso soup can be found on the menu, but it's mostly full of creative dishes that innovate beyond the classics.

Utagawa trusts his chefs to be creative, but he himself is credited with pairing Japanese fish with wine. "When you're a Japanese cook, you're taught to understand about rice and fish, but wine? [They'd say] what the hell are you doing with wine? Drink sake!" But by following his own idea of subtraction, Utagawa wanted to take sake out of the equation and try something new. That something was Burgundy red wine.

A fan of the wine, Utagawa realized that it actually paired well with sashimi. But the combination was unheard of at the time. "Sushi and red wine? Forget about it," he says. It took some major convincing, but Utagawa's idea gradually began to spread, and it's certainly no longer unheard of. "Being in America gave me the freedom to do that," he says. Distance from Japanese food gave him the perspective to build on his native cuisine.

Sushiko expanded to Chevy Chase in 2008. Five years later, its original location in Glover Park closed. Today the Chevy Chase building serves up art not only on the plate but also on the walls.

A large photo of a busy Japanese marketplace serves as the backdrop to the circular sushi bar. A beautiful stone mosaic that evokes Mount Fuji decorates a hallway. Large paintings by Omar Alhegelan put a Japanese spin on Jackson Pollock's trademark drip paintings with more negative space than Pollock favored. Paintings by Megan Duncanson portraying trees in different seasons put a Western spin on the prevalence of seasonal imagery in Japanese artwork. But Sushiko's artistic masterpiece is tucked away on the domed walls of a side room: a mural by Iona Rozeal Brown.

Brown is known for pairing unlikely forces in her work. Her two-part mural at Sushiko does just that by putting a traditional *hanami* ("cherry blossom viewing") scene in DC (Sushiko to be exact). The mural has a comic-book feel and depicts Japanese and Western characters enjoying sushi, soup, and sake on the floor at Sushiko. Gigantic cherry blossoms take the place of clouds above their heads.

Utagawa wanted to avoid what he calls the "*Kill Bill* effect" with Sushiko's decor. Instead of kitschy, stereotypical decorations, he wanted to achieve an aesthetic that embodies Japanese values. With many rooms that are beautifully but minimally decorated, Sushiko does just that. There's so much beauty to enjoy in the restaurant, but it is a far cry from cluttered.

Unlike Brown, Sushiko's pairs two things that traditionally go very well together: a great design and great food.

TABARD INN

1739 N STREET NW • WASHINGTON, DC 20036

(202) 331-8528 • TABARDINN.COM

Job Creator, Appetite Savior

*I*f you want to explore DC, Geoffrey Chaucer might suggest you begin at the Tabard Inn. In *The Canterbury Tales*, Chaucer's characters begin their pilgrimage to Canterbury at the Tabard Inn. But you don't have to go "across the pond" to visit the Tabard. There's a Tabard Inn located in Dupont Circle right here in DC.

Established in 1922 by Marie Willoughby Rogers, the Tabard Inn has been a landmark hotel, restaurant, and bar in DC since its inception. The three town houses that compose the Tabard Inn date back to the late nineteenth century. The hotel boasts thirty-eight rooms, and the restaurant and bar is famous for its brunch.

Antiques clutter the rooms of the Tabard, giving it a homey, Victorian feel. The sitting room off the restaurant features a crackling fire and a striking two-headed eagle carved in profile. The eagle sets the tone for the patriotic room, which features several military prints and portraits of George Washington. Artwork honoring our nation's beginnings is paired with artwork that showcases how far it's come, particularly one print of the Statue of Liberty wearing jeans and heels. Patterned rugs cover creaking wood floors in the dimly lit room, along with a chess table, end tables, and old Victorian couches. The restaurant achieves a more modern feel with artwork ranging in style and medium.

During World War II, seventy members of the navy's WAVES (Women Accepted for Volunteer Emergency Service) boarded at the Tabard Inn. One

of those WAVES was the brilliant Grace Murray Hopper. Hopper received a PhD in math from Yale in 1934. The WAVES sent her to the Bureau of Ships Computation Team at Harvard, where she developed the first computer, the Mark I. The U.S. Navy used Mark I, weighing five tons and measuring fifty-five feet by eight feet, from 1944 to 1959. Hopper actually coined the phrase computer "bug." The first "bug" was in fact a real moth whose presence inside the Mark I compromised its functionality.

Proprietor Marie Rogers passed away in 1970. The Tabard Inn almost closed when a developer wanted to build an eight-story office building in its place. But Fritzi and Edward Cohen stepped in.

"Edward had an office directly across the street," says Fritzi. "I had never really noticed it in particular," she continues. "It was pink. I wonder how I could not have noticed it." The husband and wife bought the pink landmark in 1975.

Fritzi and Edward both worked in public interest. Although neither had any hospitality experience, both were passionate about projects that created jobs. "Edward said the only reason you go into business is to create jobs," recalls Fritzi. And running the Tabard would provide plenty of those.

The first order of business was redecorating. They did away with the pink exterior, opting for gray-painted brick, and moved on to the interior. "In 1975 it was a huge dump," Fritzi remembers. "The whole place was this unattractive shade of greenish blue." Without much money to spend, the only option was to decorate the Tabard in a mismatched style room by room over time. "Not every room was going to be the same," says Fritzi. Over the years, she filled each room and cranny with colors, furniture, and artwork. However, "I never bought anything just to fill a space," she clarifies. "Every picture that I bought, there is a story about."

For instance, the Pocahontas Room honors Edward, who passed away in 1999. "Edward had a fascination with Pocahontas," Fritzi explains. Another sitting room features all Japanese decor, including a giant painting of women in kimonos, a woodblock wave print, and a red Buddha statue.

"It looks like an art gallery," says Fritzi. And it works. Every corner turned provides a new artistic experience.

The Tabard averages an occupancy rate of more than 90 percent. Before you book a room, be warned: there's no elevator, and there aren't any TVs. "This isn't everybody's cup of tea," Fritzi acknowledges. However, there is Wi-Fi, and for special occasions like political debates or the Super Bowl, the Tabard provides viewing opportunities.

The second order of business was to add a restaurant to the Tabard. Fritzi and Edward hired Nora Pouillon to create a menu and run the kitchen. (She would go on to open her own place, Restaurant Nora, featured earlier in this book.) Early reviewers did not favor the Tabard Inn, but the restaurant has gone on to become exceptionally popular, especially for brunch, which features the Tabard's signature cinnamon sugar doughnuts served with vanilla whipped cream. Brunch items range from a vanilla french toast topped with plum and raspberry compote to fried oysters and cheese grits. Dinner items like asparagus and goat cheese ravioli and gumbo feature local, fresh ingredients. The menu changes daily based on what's fresh, local, and in season.

The bar features small bites like a fried meatball with chili and a mushroom quesadilla. The Tabard Cocktail mixes tequila and sherry with Drambuie, orange bitters, and thyme.

Lunch is pretty business heavy. On a weekday afternoon, at least one customer in my section had military stripes, and another party discussed politics with an air of personal experience.

No matter where you're making a pilgrimage to, the Tabard Inn is a good place to start.

TASTEE DINER

7731 WOODMONT AVENUE • BETHESDA, MD 20814

(301) 652-3970 • TASTEEDINER.COM

Tasty Tastee

Ginger Daughtrey spots a woman across the street. "She's gonna come in here for her numbers," she says. Under a red hat and wearing blue eyeliner, Daughtrey works the cash register at Tastee Diner, Bethesda's go-to diner since 1935. The woman she spots coming in for her lottery tickets is one of Tastee's many regulars. "I've got customers coming here three times a day," says Tastee Diner owner Gene Wilkes. "When someone walks in, [we] know exactly what you're eating, drinking, [and] what kind of articles you like to read in the newspaper," adds Daughtrey. "People come and feel at home."

Tastee Diner opened in 1935 on Woodmont Avenue in Bethesda under Eddie Warner. Two other Tastee Diners opened in Laurel and Silver Spring. Gene Wilkes bought the Bethesda diner in 1970. "I always wanted to be in business for myself," he says. "I wanted the freedom of making my own decisions. It worked out reasonably well." It did indeed. Wilkes purchased the Laurel diner in 1976 and the Silver Spring diner in 1988. At seventy-one years old, he still owns and operates all three.

Tastee Diner is long and mostly rectangular in the traditional railway-car shape of most diners. The word "diner" comes from the "dining car" of a train. Traditional diners are prefabricated and transported to a location, mostly ready to open. Sometimes operators convert decommissioned railway cars into diners. Before railway cars, operators converted wagons into eateries.

The Laurel Tastee Diner was prefabricated by Comac and established in 1951. The Silver Spring and Bethesda Tastee Diners were constructed by the Jerry O'Mahony Diner Company, which manufactured two thousand diners from 1917 to 1941.

A long counter has seventeen maroon stools wearing their age. Booths with mini jukeboxes line the walls. The floors are checkered in black, white, and brown. On the walls hang photos of a wedding, kids in football jerseys, and countless Christmas cards.

Enlarged articles about regular Tastee customer Josh Bolten, the twenty-second White House chief of staff to George W. Bush, hang on the walls. Bolten has been quoted saying the Tastee Diner is his favorite restaurant. His mother even commissioned an artist to paint a watercolor portrait of the diner for her son. Head shots of other prominent guests hang over the counter, such as House of Representatives member Connie Marella, twenty-eighth mayor of Rockville Doug Duncan, and Maryland's attorney general Doug Gansler.

Over one booth near the entrance hangs a sign: "Reserved for WTOP." The Washington radio station uses Tastee Diner as a polling place for reactions to local news. Wilkes estimates reporters from WTOP come to the diner weekly. "They're in on Monday morning after football," he says, "or when there's a huge political event."

The Tastee Diner's a great place to gauge public reaction because its clientele runs the gamut, from high school students to doctors, lawyers, judges, and drunks late at night. In the last few years, shift manager Kyle Brake says there have been more new customers as development in Bethesda attracts new residents. Wilkes says that even prominent folks on opposite sides of political development are "all the same when they're here." They know each other and talk about football when at Tastee. Overall, Wilkes describes his customers as "a great group of folks."

Tastee customers feel comfortable at its stools and booths. Part of that is the staff. "We get to know our customers," says Wilkes. "I've probably been able to speak to over a hundred folks today." After forty-five years at Tastee, "it becomes your life," says Wilkes. "The customers become your friends."

Tastee Diner serves breakfast, lunch, and dinner. Along with traditional omelets, burgers, and sandwiches, the diner offers some rather impressive dinner items for a diner, including a sixteen-ounce T-bone steak, fried flounder, and a grilled pork chop. "People travel thirty miles to get our barbecue ribs," claims Wilkes. The diner has added some gluten-free and low-fat items for customers searching for healthy options, but it has not gotten rid of its classics. "People still desire meat loaf and mashed potatoes and gravy," says Wilkes. "We've got both."

The biggest change in recent years comes not for the customers but for the staff at the hands of Obamacare. WTOP has gotten an earful from Wilkes about his opposition to Obamacare because it will negatively affect his staff. He worries he'll have to cut back on staff and shorten some employees' hours to meet government mandates. "Sick leave, those things should be at the discretion of the operator," Wilkes argues. "While the intention is good, the folks that are making the decisions have never run a business, never worried about a bottom line," he says. "They don't have to worry about, 'Can I pay the bill? Make a profit?' I believe in taking care of people obviously . . . at our own discretion."

Other than the struggles to adhere to new government regulations, the Tastee Diner's greatest challenge was a fire in 2002. "It was pretty devastating for all of us," says Daughtrey. The diner closed for about three months. But Wilkes arranged for Bethesda employees to work at Tastee's other locations while the Bethesda diner underwent repairs. "He takes care of his people," Daughtrey says of Wilkes.

Head over to Tastee and let the staff take care of you.

THE TOMBS

1226 36TH STREET NW • WASHINGTON, DC 20007

(202) 337-6668 • TOMBS.COM

By a Hoya, for Hoyas

In T. S. Eliot's poem "Bustopher Jones: The Cat about Town," a portly cat enjoys meals throughout London. Eliot wrote, "If he looks full of gloom then he's lunched at the Tomb." This line inspired the name for the Tombs, but luckily, patrons of this Georgetown staple won't share Bustopher's disappointed reaction.

The Tombs is a classic college bar and restaurant steps from Georgetown University's campus. Follow the red cobblestone to Prospect and 36th Street and walk through a high green archway to enter this basement eatery.

Outside, a blue-and-white oar hangs above the entrance, and inside, oars decorate brick walls to establish a rowing theme. Framed photos of Georgetown sports teams hang above red booths and glossy wooden tables. Historical navy recruitment posters serve as a backdrop to the rectangular bar. Servers and bartenders sport button-down shirts and bow ties to complete the restaurant's preppy atmosphere.

During his time as a student at Georgetown, founder Richard McCooey served as president of the Yard (also known as the student body). When he opened the Tombs in 1962, he essentially became the president of student social life: By day, you are sure to see students sharing a meal with a professor, and by night, expect to rub elbows with undergraduates embracing their newly legal right to imbibe. From Monday Country Nights to Tuesday Trivia Nights and daily specials, the Tombs is "a very vital organ of

the college experience" at Georgetown, according to general manager Rich Kaufman.

So ingrained in student culture is the Tombs that some seniors take the 99 Day Challenge: those who visit the Tombs every day for the last 99 days of school are inducted into the 99 Days Club. Since the Class of 1999 started the club, thousands have been inducted. Look for their names engraved on the walls, exemplifying the sense of community that McCooey hoped the Tombs would foster.

Classic American food is moderately priced. From hamburgers to steak and salmon, the menu is diverse and everyone is sure to find something they'll like. My personal favorite is the Hoya Salad: a giant platter of lettuce topped with tangy chicken, vegetables, cheese, and tortilla chips atop a bubbly pizza crust.

Complimentary coffee cake adds a sweet touch to the brunch menu, which offers common items like french toast and twists on staples, like the autumn squash omelet and pumpkin waffles with cinnamon whipped cream. Pastry chef Ryan Westover's desserts offer sweet after-dinner options, and the menu reflects the restaurant's participation in the Clyde's farm-to-table program, which brings fruits and vegetables from local farms to your table.

If you want to avoid a packed crowd, leave before 9:30 p.m., when the space becomes a twenty-one-and-over crowd. But if you want the quintessential college bar experience, find someone with a stamp on his/her forehead, signaling a twenty-first birthday, and buy him one of the Tombs' colorfully titled shots.

If you have a sudden urge to dig out your fanny pack and shoulder pads, it's probably because the Tombs reminds you of the 1985 brat pack movie *St. Elmo's Fire*. The titular bar in the film, which follows a group of recent Georgetown alums as they navigate postgraduate life, is based on the Tombs.

If you feel like working off the beer you've just downed, take a little jaunt outside and find the *Exorcist* steps across the street. The 1973 horror flick filmed a scene on these very steep steps in which Father Karras crashes out a window and tumbles downward. Even before *The Exorcist*, these steps were nicknamed the Hitchcock steps because there was something inherently spooky about them. By day, you're more likely to find undergrads using them for exercise, and by night, tipsy couples have been known to escape the Tombs for a make-out session on the steps.

If you're in the mood for a more elegant—and much more expensive—dining experience, hike upstairs to 1789, a fine dining restaurant that Richard McCooey also opened in 1962. You won't find many undergrads enjoying the cuisine, but you may rub shoulders with some of DC's most important residents. President Obama took German chancellor Angela Merkel to 1789 for dinner in 2011. The Tombs' sister restaurant gets its name from an important year in the neighborhood's history. In 1789, not only did the United States adopt the Constitution, but archbishop John Carroll purchased the land on which the restaurant stands as part of the future Georgetown University. Unlike the Tombs, which pulses at all hours, 1789 only serves dinner.

"[McCooey's] vision was really a place for Georgetown parents, faculty, and neighbors to have a great meal, which was 1789, but also for students to have a beer and a burger," explains Kaufman of the Tombs and its upstairs neighbor.

McCooey sold the Tombs and 1789 to Clyde's Restaurant Group in 1985 but remained very involved with the establishments until his death in 2014.

The friendly, cozy pub atmosphere of the Tombs is inviting and sure to please. Whether you're looking for a brunch spot after church, a casual dinner setting, or a night to relive your youth, the Tombs has what you're looking for. If Bustopher Jones had happened upon *this* tomb, he'd say, "Hoya Saxa."

THE TUNE INN

331 PENNSYLVANIA AVENUE SE • WASHINGTON, DC 20003

(202) 543-2725

Deep-Fried Capitol Hill

The booty trend has made its way into the animal kingdom. At least at the Tune Inn. A stuffed deer rump hangs on the wall above the bathroom of this beloved neighborhood bar, shot by the bar's owner, Lisa Nardelli. The deer butt is joined by other stuffed animals, including a black bear holding a beer can shot by Lisa's husband, a fox rocking a handkerchief, squirrels, muskrats, and more deer hunted by Joe Nardelli, the original owner.

Stuffed mounts holding guns clutter the narrow bar's wood paneling along with more guns, fake fish, trophies, ducks, and framed pictures. A chandelier that looks like a web of antlers hangs from the rafters.

Joe Nardelli, the youngest of nine children in a large Italian family, worked as a coal miner in West Virginia before moving to Washington, DC. In 1955, he bought the building that housed the Tune Inn. It became a family business when "West Virginia Joe" passed it down to his son Tony, who passed it down to his daughter Lisa.

The building itself has a storied past. Before it was a bar, it was a candy store, and before it was the *current* bar, it was one of the first bars to open in the District after Prohibition ended in 1933. But there were still strict rules regulating the alcohol industry. Lisa discovered a staircase that had been covered with drywall where servers brought up one bottle of liquor at a time from the basement to acquiesce to the strict regulations.

The rectangular space hosts a long bar and two columns of comfortable, black booths at white tables.

The Tune Inn ropes people from all walks of life in the door. Police officers, night nurses, and politicians are treated alike. Bartenders greet regulars by name and give politicians their space. Former attorney general Janet Reno used to hit up the Tune Inn for a burger in a low-key pair of jeans. She wrote a note now framed on the wall that says, "Thank you for the best hamburger in town." Several married couples have met at the Tune Inn, including Lisa and her husband. Democrat James Carville famously *tried* to take his future Republican wife, Mary, to the Tune Inn for their first date, but it was so crowded that they had to relocate.

But famous folk are not what makes the Tune Inn great. It's regulars like the one that holds Easter egg hunts in the restaurant and buys Easter hats for his friends. Or another that proposed at the Tune. So committed to the establishment are its regulars that when a kitchen fire badly damaged the Tune in 2011, many showed up to help with its cleanup and fund-raise for its restoration. The fire damaged many of the animals mounted on the walls. Their restoration set the Tune Inn back about $10,000. But without its taxidermy theme, the walls at the Tune Inn would have felt naked.

The Tune wasn't always so safe and friendly. In its early days under Joe, it wasn't uncommon for several fights to break out a day. In the 1970s, Joe suffered six gunshot wounds while being robbed nearby. Drugs and violence plagued the neighborhood the following decades.

In the 1990s, the *Washington Post* published an article in which ten-year-olds had started to plan their own funerals. In an article for *The Atlantic* from 2000, neighborhood resident Jim Myers writes about the many shootings he witnessed near his home. In 1989, with more than four hundred homicides, DC officially became the United States' murder capital. But as revitalization efforts improved DC's neighborhood, including Capitol Hill, the city became much safer. In 2014, the city recorded only 105 homicides.

The Tune Inn sits on a tree-lined block that has become, in my opinion, somewhat adorable over the years.

Lisa ran the Tune Inn with Tony until he passed away in 2006. Afterward, the Tune Inn threw a party honoring his memory.

The food is cheap, greasy, and classic American. The Tune serves breakfast all day. Pick from Texas French Toast (everything's bigger in Texas), the cream cheese–stuffed omelet, or biscuits and gravy. The Tune Inn gets its sausage patties delivered from a local farm in Virginia. You might spy shift workers having their breakfast at 5 p.m. or their own personal happy hour at 9 a.m.

For lunch, prepare to deep-fat-fry your esophagus with the mac and cheese wedges (topped with salsa ranch dressing) or the chicken balls (stuffed with blue cheese and hot sauce and then topped with more blue cheese). The dessert menu even includes a fried cheesecake.

Greasy appetizers like mozzarella sticks and beer-battered fried mushrooms with salsa and ranch dressing are sure to satisfy. The corned beef hash, diced with green peppers, onions, and potatoes, is also quite popular.

Classic sandwiches and burgers fill out the lunch and dinner menus, along with corn dogs, pork chops, a fish fry basket, and shrimp fettuccine Alfredo. If you don't want to completely abandon your diet, choose from several healthy salads such as the salmon Caesar salad, topped with walnuts and sun-dried tomatoes or cranberries.

If you like staring into a deer's eyes while you chase a beer with a shot or dig into a deep-fried dinner, head for the Tune Inn.

TREASURE TROVE JEWELERS

1305 G STREET NW • WASHINGTON, DC 20005

(202) 628-4653 • TREASURETROVEJEWELERS.COM

Frost Yourselves

*I*n the same store in the same week, two men buy engagement rings. One buys a ring for $12,500, the other for $249. Here at Treasure Trove Jewelers, sales have run the full spectrum since 1948.

The man with the cheaper ring may be on to something: an Emory University study concluded that higher costs of engagement rings and weddings correlated with higher chances for divorce. According to the study, the sweet spot for an engagement ring is between $500 and $2,000. Cheaper weddings also created less stress to start off a marriage, perhaps yielding greater success rates. The expectation of a *diamond* engagement ring is a relatively recent one. Before the 1940s in the Western world, only one in ten engagement rings contained a diamond. By 2000, 80 percent did. Weddings have gotten bigger and more expensive as time goes on, particularly as people marry later and later with more cash at their disposal than in years past. But even if you have lots to spend on a ring, at least one study says maybe you shouldn't. And at Treasure Trove, you can buy quality jewelry at a reasonable price.

A sign at the family-run jewelry store hammers home this idea:

WE AT TREASURE TROVE WOULD LIKE TO REMIND YOU:

1) OUR JEWELRY JUST LOOKS EXPENSIVE

2) THE BITTERNESS OF POOR QUALITY REMAINS LONG AFTER THE SWEETNESS OF LOW PRICE IS FORGOTTEN

The small store features cases of watches, necklaces, rings, cufflinks, stones, and bracelets.

Marc Broder runs Treasure Trove with his brother, David, and sister-in-law, Susan. Marc and David's parents opened the store after World War II. The store originated as a gift shop that sold jewelry, but after a fire in the early 1960s, the store transitioned into a full-on jewelry store selling gold and diamonds.

"I had no formal education [in jewelry]," reveals Marc. "I've been doing this since I was seven years old. I guess through osmosis I picked it up." His brother David is the store's wedding specialist who has extensive knowl-edge of engagement rings.

"We're not an expensive jewelry store," says Marc. "We're not compet-ing against the real fancy-pants [stores]. We have fine jewelry but we're not expensive." The average watch goes for $150, and the average engagement ring they sell is a single carat. The store also offers items on layaway with no interest, a bargain that brings customers in the door. On more than one occasion, after the original buyer passed away, customers have come in to pick up items that have been on layaway for a long time. One woman even picked up something her husband had on layaway for him to wear it in his casket. "So he could wear it into eternity," recalls Marc.

The store's clientele has changed dramatically over the years. In the store's early years, pimps, hustlers, and members of DC's "underworld" fre-quented Treasure Trove. But after the 1980s, business from those figures fizzled. "Our clientele has evolved every five years," estimates Marc.

Today the majority of the store's business comes from African-American women buying jewelry for themselves, young professionals, and engaged couples. "Thank goodness the young folks are getting married," says Marc.

It's been hard for Treasure Trove to stay in business. "The Internet has really, really changed this business," says Marc. "About five, six times a day I get people coming in here with watches they bought online." Marc used to fix watches for free, but now that customers are bringing in watches they bought elsewhere, he charges a simple $10 fee. Internet jewelry purchases don't make sense to Marc. "To me, jewelry is a touchy-feely product. I don't know how anybody could buy anything without trying it on."

Unlike many jewelry stores, Treasure Trove manufactures more than 90 percent of its mounted jewelry. "By eliminating middlemen and wholesalers, we have drastically lowered our costs by up to 50 percent," says Marc.

Treasure Trove carries an inventory of about $125,000. Some jewelry stores opt to carry inventory they don't own, paying for it over months or years. But at Treasure Trove, everything is owned within about thirty days of acquiring it. Treasure Trove offers very low markups. Their prices are often lower than jewelry that's been significantly marked *down* at large department stores.

"It is indeed a challenge to stay in business," laments Marc. The store once had six employees but now has four, one of whom is part-time. The store used to generate $1.5 million a year in sales but now generates about $750,000.

To bring in extra revenue, Treasure Trove has started a currency exchange program. The store also buys scrap gold from customers and gives them credit toward new purchases.

Many customers at Treasure Trove have been purchasing jewelry here for years. Marc, David, and Susan greet these regulars by name. "[Our] service has made us a favorite of knowledgeable jewelry buyers for fifty years," says Marc. Despite intense competition from department stores, this independent jeweler has managed to frost customers for half a century. If you're looking to support a local, family-owned business and get a great deal on high-quality jewelry, 1305 G Street marks the spot for this treasure trove.

TRIO/FOX & HOUNDS

1537 17TH STREET NW • WASHINGTON, DC 20036

(202) 232-6305 • TRIODC.COM

Good Food

*H*ello, can I buy some good weather from Fort Lauderdale?" Mourad Benjelloun greets George Mallios on the phone. The current owner of Trio is calling up the former owner, but it hardly feels like business. They laugh, they praise one another, they share a common affection for the restaurant they've both called home.

Trio stands on the corner of 17th and Q. A sign promising "GOOD FOOD" in capital red letters tells it like it is. Two green awnings stretch in different directions, creating outside seating in a right angle. Inside, it's really two places in one: a restaurant, Trio, and a bar, Fox & Hounds. Inside, Martin Luther King has had lunch, and Chelsea Clinton's cried over an ex.

In 1940, three Greek waiters joined forces to create a luncheonette on this corner. The trio converted a pharmacy into a modest lunch counter and named it after themselves.

In 1950, Greek immigrants Peter and Helen Mallios bought the restaurant. Their son, George, became the heartbeat of Trio until he retired two years ago and passed the reins to Benjelloun, a twenty-year veteran of Trio.

At thirteen, Peter Mallios traveled by ship to the United States all alone. Without anyone to claim responsibility for him, the authorities sent him right back. As soon as he could make the trip again, he wised up: he called out "Uncle!" to a stranger and disappeared into the company of no one in particular. His moxie paid off. He made a life for himself in the United States. In 1928, he married Helen, a fellow Greek immigrant, and in 1940,

they moved from Pennsylvania to Washington, DC. In 1950, they purchased Trio.

"I was in high school at the time, so I worked basically Friday night and Saturday," says George. "Little by little [my father] asked me to help him more and more." After college at George Washington University, George longed for more responsibility. But Peter told him, "You stand here at the cash register. I do everything else." But George had bigger plans for his life after serving in the navy. He told his father, "Pop, don't sell the Trio. When I get back from the navy, I want to be your partner." In 1960, father and son did just that. A short time later, George's brother-in-law joined them. And just like that, the Trio had a new trio at its helm.

In 1967, Trio expanded to include Fox & Hounds, an adjoining bar that shares its kitchen. "That became a very happy hangout," says George. A chandelier featuring four foxes hangs from the ceiling of the small bar, which has served the likes of Anderson Cooper, Drew Barrymore, and many congressmen and women.

In 1975, after the law no longer prohibited sidewalk cafes, Trio added one of the first outdoor cafes in the capital. "It was so popular, we expanded," says George. He and his partners increased the outdoor seating to wrap around the entire property, as it does today in a large "L."

In 1968, riots swept DC up in flames after Martin Luther King Jr. was shot. "You could see the smoke," remembers George, who was at the restaurant when the riots began. "Lock your doors, send your employees home, [and] get your customers out of here," he recalls of Trio's response. "We went home not knowing if we [would have] a restaurant the next day. Fortunately, we were spared."

But much of DC was not, and the city went into a depression. Luckily, the Trio was able to weather the economic struggles of many people moving away. Part of Trio's ability to sustain was its simple approach. "Good food at a reasonable price," says George. "That's pretty much it. What more would you want?" he laughs.

Only recently has the Trio begun to change. In order to keep up with DC's increasingly fierce culinary competition and keep up with clients' changing palates, Maraud has made some modest changes to the menu. That includes bringing vegetables and eggs from local farms to your plate and switching to all-natural, hormone-free meats. He also has put into motion a simpler menu that reflects customers' all-time favorites. Those favorites include meat loaf, fish-and-chips, turkey potpie, chicken Marsala, and eggplant parmigiana.

Benjelloun has also remodeled the restaurant, making it more upscale and comfortable than in its former days as a diner.

Over the years, breakfast business has steeply declined. "Starbucks everywhere killed all that business," George laments. He sees the fifty-and-over crowds at breakfast but hopes to draw younger people into breakfast in the future.

Benjelloun never expected to be at Trio for more than two decades. Before Trio, he worked in fine dining but tired of the uptight constraints and perfectionism of his former work spots. A friend introduced him to George, who offered him a managerial position. "I was thinking, let's do it for some time. Two or three months and see what happens." That turned into twenty years. "I never quit because of George," he says. "You see that man over there?" he points to a picture. It's a snapshot of a white-haired George shoveling a mountain of snow outside Trio. With deep affection and respect, Benjelloun regales me with tales of George's kind treatment of employees over the years. They speak often, and Benjelloun keeps George informed about developments at the Trio.

Benjelloun's business card says "owner," but he doesn't like that title. "The customer is the owner," he insists. He's "just" the operator. So if you'd like to be treated like an owner without doing any heavy lifting, head for the corner of 17th and Q.

ZIEGFELD'S/SECRETS

1824 HALF STREET SW • WASHINGTON, DC 20024

(202) 863-0670 • ZIEGFELDS.COM

The Secret's Out

The ironic downside to a nation that has become more equal for LGBTQ Americans is the dwindling number of gay bars. As gay marriage has become legal nationwide, TV and films feature more gay characters, and gay men and women are embraced by mainstream culture, members of the LGBTQ community are welcomed in all sorts of bars. "Straight" bars are even hosting queer events. Online dating is also to blame for the decline of the same-sex establishment. You don't have to go to a gay bar to find gay people. They're "out" in the real world and easy to find online.

But one gay bar that's survived for more than forty years is Ziegfeld's/ Secrets. Since 1970, Ziegfeld's has featured drag performances on the first floor on Friday and Saturday nights and nude dancing upstairs at Secrets Wednesday through Sunday.

Bouncers go over three rules before entering: (1) no touching dancers between their upper thighs and hips, (2) no photography upstairs, and (3) no screaming. Security is required to respond to any screaming, so "woooo!" girls need to keep their excited cries in check.

On the first floor, aka Ziegfeld's, blue, green, and pink lights shine on tables surrounding a spacious dance floor and stage. Techno music blasts remixes of J. Lo and La Roux. Televisions play erotic footage of naked men at photo shoots. Bartenders serve drinks shirtless. A DJ shows off his muscles in a tight black tank top while he spins in the back.

Upstairs at Secrets, men wearing nothing but sneakers and tube socks (on their feet) dance on top of the bar and on several stages throughout

the floor. Gluteal muscles flex, penises rotate in circles, and one man dancing on the bar even does gymnastics flips. You're allowed to touch and be touched. On a Saturday night, one dancer crawls over to a man sitting in a chair and begins to give him a lap dance. Another man dancing on the bar reaches for an onlooker's hand and guides it up his taut torso.

At 11:30 p.m., many of the men and women—most of them here for bachelorette parties—gravitate back downstairs for the night's first of two drag shows. Miss Ella Fitzgerald, a thirty-four-year veteran of Ziegfeld's, emerges in a sparkly dress and an overcoat of gold ruffles. Fitzgerald works as a makeup artist and hairdresser during the day and then transforms into Ella Fitzgerald, the "Hurricane on Heels," at night.

Ella shows off her impressive voice with a jazzy rendition of Pink's "Get This Party Started." Her glittery headpiece is ten times more fabulous than any hat seen at the royal wedding. Ella gets everyone to repeat "Hey, bitch!" which sounds decidedly different than anytime Jesse Pinkman ever said it.

She asks the crowd, "How many people like penis?" and the gay men and bachelorettes respond with affirmative shouts. Off to the side, a man translates Fitzgerald's words into sign language. Ella hands the reins over to a series of performers who lip-synch tunes by Ariana Grande, Whitney Houston, Beyoncé, and more. Known as "The Ladies of Illusion," all the drag queens' outfits are an ode to sparkle, ruffles, and wigs.

Drag performances have a long, rich history dating back to Ancient Greece, when the law forbade women to perform onstage. In the 1500s and 1600s, British theater famously employed drag performances. Shakespeare used cross-dressing as a common plot device in his writing. Japanese Kabuki theater also employed men in female roles through the 1800s. As gay men came out of the closet in the twentieth century, drag performances became associated with homosexuality, an illegal and vilified practice in many states. To get around laws prohibiting drag performances, some performers wore male clothing underneath their female outfits.

In drag culture, performers are related in "families" of grandmothers, mothers, and daughters, much like in fraternities or sororities. Historically, for LGBTQ members who've been disowned by their biological families, drag families provide a much-needed support system.

Allen Carroll opened Ziegfeld's in 1970 with his late partner, Chris Jansen. In a true meet-cute, their eyes met at a red traffic light. They made a coffee date, and that spawned a sixteen-year romantic relationship followed by a lifelong friendship and business partnership. Jansen passed away in 2007.

Today, Carroll owns both Ziegfeld's and Phase 1, the country's oldest lesbian bar in DC, as well as Phase 1 of Dupont, a dance club in Dupont Circle.

Don't let the seedy drive here fool you. Located down a dark road past construction trucks in dirt lots a few blocks from the Nationals stadium, Z/S feels far removed from anything and even a little scary. But inside, that couldn't be further from the truth. Z/S is exceptionally clean and well lit. Even when packed, the bar is so spacious that you never feel unsafe or claustrophobic.

Ziegfeld's almost disappeared a few years ago. After operating for more than thirty years, the city forced Z/S and several other gay clubs nearby to close their doors in order to build the Nationals stadium in 2006. Most of the gay clubs that had once been clustered together could not find a new place to reopen. Glorious Health Club, Follies, and Heat are just a few that eminent domain killed. Luckily, Ziegfeld's/Secrets reopened after a three-year hiatus.

The clientele is thankful. One bartender working his second-ever shift tells me he used to go to the old Ziegfeld's when he was an eighteen-year-old just coming out of the closet. A thirtysomething couple tells me they come here three or four times a month.

With that kind of dedicated clientele, Ziegfeld's/Secrets has been doing something right for decades.

Appendix A

FEATURED PLACES BY CATEGORY

Bakery:
Catania Bakery, 27

Bars:
Stetson's, 185
The Raven Grill, 167

Bookstores:
Idle Time Books, 69
Kramerbooks & Afterwords Café, 83

Comic Book Store:
Big Planet Comics, 7

Deli:
Parkway Deli, 143

Diners:
Florida Avenue Grill, 57
Tastee Diner, 199

Hot Dogs:
Ben's Chili Bowl, 1

Hotel Restaurants/Bars:
Off the Record, 123
Quill, 163
Round Robin Bar, 175
Tabard Inn, 195

Ice Cream:
Frozen Dairy Bar Eatery, 61

Jazz Clubs:
Blues Alley, 13
Bohemian Caverns, 17

Jewelry:
Treasure Trove Jewelers, 211

LGBTQ:
Ziegfeld's/Secrets, 219

Market/Specialty Food Store:
A. Litteri, 93

Record Store:
Joe's Record Paradise, 79

Appendix B

FEATURED PLACES BY NEIGHBORHOOD

Appendix C

FEATURED PLACES BY YEAR OF ORIGIN

1958: Ben's Chili Bowl, 1
1960: The Monocle, 105
1962: The Tombs, 203
1963: Clyde's, 37
1963: Parkway Deli, 143
1965: Blues Alley, 13
1970: Portofino, 153
1970: Ziegfeld's/Secrets, 219
1972: The Palm, 139
1974: Joe's Record Paradise, 79
1974: The Dubliner, 45
1976: Kramerbooks & Afterwords Café, 83
1976: The Prime Rib, 159
1976: Sushiko, 189
1978: Peking Gourmet Inn, 147
1979: Restaurant Nora, 171
1980: Stetson's, 185
1981: Idle Time Books, 69
1981: The Mad Hatter, 97
1983: Filomena, 53
1983: Lauriol Plaza, 87
1986: Big Planet Comics, 7
1987: Nam Viet, 115
1988: The Bombay Club, 21
1990: Chinatown Expressm 33

Index